RAMANA MAHARSHI

AND THE

PATH OF SELF-KNOWLEDGE

A Biography
by
ARTHUR OSBORNE

Foreword
by
Dr. S. RADHAKRISHNAN
Vice-President of India

SRI RAMANASRAMAM
Tiruvannamalai
2002

© Sri Ramanasramam

First Edition : 1997
Second Edition : 2002
             2000 copies

Price: Rs. 70/-
CC No: 1052

Published by
V.S. Ramanan
President, Board of Trustees
Sri Ramanasramam
Tiruvannamalai 606 603
Tamil Nadu
INDIA
Tel: 91-4175-37292
Fax: 91-4175-37491
Email: alagamma@vsnl.com
Website: www.ramana-maharshi.org

ISBN   81-88018-11-2

Designed and typeset at
Sri Ramanasramam

Printed by
Kartik Offset Printers
Chennai 600 015

PUBLISHER'S NOTE

Since the printing of this work as an Ashram publication in 1997 there has been demand for a reprint.

A second edition has therefore been brought out, also utilising the opportunity to effect some improvement.

The improvement consists in the addition of illustrations appropriate to the contents of each chapter.

TIRUVANNAMALAI
15 FEBRUARY 2002

V.S. RAMANAN
PUBLISHER

Preface

In writing this book I have tried to make the meaning clear without using more foreign words than necessary. However, every language contains words which have no direct equivalent in another, and every science, spiritual as well as physical, has technical terms which scarcely admit of translation. Therefore it was necessary to use a certain number of Sanskrit and other words. These have been explained in the text, but for easy reference and for an approximate idea of their pronunciation, a glossary has been added. Since it is intended to help the general reader in his understanding of the book, I have not given simple dictionary definitions but rather an idea of the sense in which a word is used and of the doctrinal implications it carries.

ARTHUR OSBORNE

FOREWORD

by Dr. S. Radhakrishnan, Vice-President of India

I am glad to write this short foreword to Mr. Osborne's account of the life and teaching of Sri Ramana Maharshi. It has a special relevance to our age with its dominant mood of wistful reluctant scepticism. We are given here a religion of the spirit which enables us to liberate ourselves from dogmas and superstitions, rituals and ceremonies and live as free spirits. The essence of all religion is an inner personal experience, an individual relationship with the Divine. It is not worship so much as a quest. It is a way of becoming, of liberation.

The well-known Greek aphorism 'Know thyself' is akin to the *Upanishad* precept *atmanam viddhi*, know the Self. By a process of abstraction we get behind the layers of body, mind and intellect and reach the Universal Self, "the true light which lighteth every man that cometh into the world". "To attain the Good, we must ascend to the highest state and fixing our gaze thereon, lay aside the garments we donned when descending here below; just as, in the Mysteries, those who are admitted to penetrate into the inner recesses of the sanctuary, after having purified themselves, lay aside every garment and advance stark naked."[1] We sink into the measureless being that is without limitation or determination. It is pure being in which one thing is not opposed to another. There is no being to which the subject opposes himself. He identifies himself with all things and events

---

[1] Plotinus: *Enneads*, I, vi, 6.

as they happen. Reality fills the self as it is no longer barred by preferences or aversions, likes or dislikes. These can no more act as a distorting medium.

The child is much nearer the vision of the Self. We must become as little children before we can enter into the realm of truth. This is why we are required to put aside the sophistication of the learned. The need for being born again is insisted on. It is said that the wisdom of babes is greater than that of scholars.

Sri Ramana Maharshi gives us the outlines of a religion based on the Indian Scriptures which is essentially spiritual without ceasing to be rational and ethical.

S. RADHAKRISHNAN

CONTENTS

LIST OF ILLUSTRATIONS

1
EARLY YEARS

ARUDRA DARSHAN, the day of the 'Sight of Siva', is observed with great devotion by *Saivites*, for it commemorates the occasion when Siva manifested himself to His devotees as Nataraja, that is in the cosmic dance of creation and dissolution of the universe. On this day in 1879 it was still dusk when Siva's devotees in the little town of Tiruchuzhi in the Tamil land of South India left their houses and padded barefoot along the dusty roads to the temple tank, for tradition demands that they should bathe at daybreak. The red glow of sunrise fell upon the brown torsos of the men, clad only in a *dhoti*, a white cotton cloth wrapped round the body from the waist down, and flashed in the deep reds and golds of the women's saris as they descended the stone steps of the large square tank and immersed themselves in the water. There was a nip in the air, for the festival fell in December, but they are hardy folk. Some few changed under trees or in houses near the tank but most waited for the rising sun to dry them and proceeded, dripping as they were, to the little town's ancient temple, hymned long ago by Sundaramurthi Swami, one of the sixty-three *Saivite* poet-saints of the Tamil land.

The image of Siva in the temple was garlanded with flowers and taken in procession throughout the day and night, with noise of drum and conch and chanting of sacred song. It was one o'clock at night when the processions ended, but still Arudra Darshan because the Hindu day stretches from dawn to dawn, not from midnight to midnight. The idol of Siva re-entered the temple just as the child Venkataraman, in whom Siva was to be manifested as Sri Ramana, entered the world in the house of Sundaram Ayyar and his wife Alagammal. A Hindu festival varies with the phase of the moon, like the Western Easter, and in this year Arudra Darshan fell on December 29th, so that the child was born a little later, both in time of day and year, than the divine child of Bethlehem nearly two thousand years before. The same coincidence marked the end of earthly life also, for Sri Ramana left his body on the evening of April 14th, a little later in time and date than Good Friday afternoon. Both times are profoundly appropriate. Midnight and the winter solstice are the time when the sun is beginning to bring back light to the world, and at the spring equinox day has equalled night and is beginning to exceed it.

After starting life as an accountant's clerk on the salary, ridiculously small even for those days, of two rupees a month, Sundaram Ayyar had set up for himself as a petition writer and then, after some years, obtained permission to practise as an uncertified pleader, that is a sort of rural lawyer. He had prospered and had built the house[1] in which the child was born, making it commodious enough for one side to be reserved for guests. It was not only that he was sociable and hospitable, but also because he took it on himself to house official visitors and newcomers to the town — which made him a person of civic importance and doubtless reacted favourably on his professional work.

Successful as he was, a strange destiny overhung the family. It is said that a wandering ascetic once stopped to beg food at the house of one of their forebears and, on being refused, turned on him and pronounced that thenceforth one out of every generation of his descendants would wander and beg his food. Curse or blessing, the pronouncement was fulfilled. One of Sundaram Ayyar's paternal uncles had donned the ochre robe and left home with staff and water-pot; his elder brother had gone ostensibly to visit a neighbouring place and from there slipped away as a *sanyasin*, renouncing the world.

There seemed nothing strange about Sundaram Ayyar's own family. Venkataraman grew up a normal, healthy boy. He was sent for awhile to the local school and then, when he was eleven, to a school in Dindigul. He had a brother, Nagaswami two years his senior. Six years after him came a third son, Nagasundaram, and two years later a daughter, Alamelu. A happy, well-to-do middle-class family.

When Venkataraman was twelve, Sundaram Ayyar died and the family was broken up. The children went to live with

---

[1] This house has now been acquired by the Ashram. Daily *puja* (ritualistic worship) is performed there and it is kept open as a place of pilgrimage for devotees.

their paternal uncle, Subbier, who had a house[1] in the nearby city of Madura. Venkataraman was sent first to Scott's Middle School there and then to the American Mission High School. There was no sign of his ever becoming a scholar. He was the athletic, out-of-doors type of boy and it was football, wrestling and swimming, that appealed to him. His one asset, so far as school goes, was an amazingly retentive memory which covered up laziness by enabling him to repeat a lesson from hearing it once read out.

The only unusual thing about him in his boyhood years was his abnormally deep sleep. Devaraja Mudaliar, a devotee, relates in his diary how he described it in a conversation at the Ashram many years later on seeing a relative entering the hall.

"Seeing you reminds me of something that happened in Dindigul when I was a boy. Your uncle, Periappa Seshayyar, was then living there. Some function was going on in the house and everyone attended it and then in the night went to the temple. I was left alone in the house. I was sitting reading in the front room, but after a while I locked the front door and fastened the windows and went to sleep. When they returned from the temple no amount of shouting or banging at the door or window would wake me. At last they managed to open the door with a key from the house opposite, and then they tried to wake me up by beating me. All the boys beat me to their heart's content, and your uncle did too, but without effect. I knew nothing about it till they told me in the morning. . . . The same

---

[1] This is the house in which Sri Bhagavan attained realization. It has been acquired by the Ashram and a portrait of Sri Bhagavan installed there. It is kept as a place of pilgrimage for devotees.

sort of thing happened to me in Madura also. The boys didn't dare touch me when I was awake but if they had any grudge against me they would come when I was asleep and carry me wherever they liked and beat me as much as they liked and then put me back to bed and I would know nothing about it till they told me next morning."

Sri Bhagavan attributed no significance to this except sound health. Sometimes also he would lie in a sort of half-sleep at night. It may be that both states were foreshadowings of the spiritual awakening: the deep sleep as the ability, albeit still dark and negative, to abandon the mind and plunge deep beyond thought, and the half-sleep as the ability to observe oneself objectively as a witness.

We have no photograph of Sri Bhagavan in his boyhood years. He has told us in his usual picturesque style, full of laughter, how a group photograph was taken and he was made to hold a heavy tome to look studious, but a fly settled on him and just as the photograph was taken he raised his arm to brush it off. However, it has not been possible to find a copy of this and presumably none remains.

The first premonition of dawn was a foreglow from Arunachala. The schoolboy Venkataraman had read no religious theory. He knew only that Arunachala was a very sacred place and it must have been a presentiment of his destiny that shook him. One day he met an elderly relative whom he had known in Tiruchuzhi and asked him where he was coming from. The old man replied, "From Arunachala." And the sudden realization that the holy hill was a real, tangible place on earth that men could visit overwhelmed Venkataraman with awe so that he could only stammer out: "What! From Arunachala? Where is that?"

The relative, wondering in his turn at the ignorance of callow youth, explained that Arunachala is Tiruvannamalai.

Sri Bhagavan referred to this later in the first of his *Eight Stanzas to Arunachala.*

> "Hearken! It stands as an insentient hill. Its action is mysterious, past human understanding. From the age of innocence it had shone in my mind that Arunachala was something of surpassing grandeur, but even when I came to know through another that it was the same as Tiruvannamalai I did not realize its meaning. When it drew me up to it, stilling the mind, and I came close I saw it stand unmoving."

This took place in November 1895, shortly before his sixteenth birthday by European computation, his seventeenth by Hindu. The second premonition came soon after. This time it was provoked by a book. Again it was a wave of bewildering joy at perceiving that the Divine can be made manifest on earth. His uncle had borrowed a copy of the *Periapuranam*, the life stories of the sixty-three Tamil Saints. Venkataraman picked it up and, as he read, was overwhelmed with ecstatic wonder that such faith, such love, such divine fervour was possible, that there had been such beauty in human life. The tales of renunciation leading to Divine Union inspired him with awe and emulation. Something greater than all dreamlands, greater than all ambition, was here proclaimed real and possible, and the revelation thrilled him with blissful gratitude.

From this time on the current of awareness which Sri Bhagavan and his devotees designate 'meditation' began to awaken in him. Not awareness of anything by any one, being beyond the duality of subject and object, but a state of blissful consciousness transcending both the physical and mental plane and yet compatible with full use of the physical and mental faculties.

Sri Bhagavan has told with a characteristic simplicity how this awareness began to awaken in him during his visits to the Meenakshi Temple at Madura. He said, "At first I thought it was some kind of fever, but I decided, if so it is a pleasant fever, so let it stay."

2
AWAKENING

THIS CURRENT of awareness, fostered by continual effort, grows ever stronger and more constant until finally it leads to Self-realization, to *sahaja samadhi*, the state in which pure blissful awareness is constant and uninterrupted and yet without impeding the normal perceptions and activities of life. It is rare indeed for this communion to be attained during the life on earth. In the case of Sri Bhagavan it occurred only a few months later and with no quest, no striving, no conscious preparation. He himself has described it.

"It was about six weeks before I left Madura for good that the great change in my life took place. It was quite sudden. I was sitting alone in a room on the first floor of my uncle's house. I seldom had any sickness, and on that day there was nothing wrong with my health, but a sudden violent fear of death overtook me. There was nothing in my state of health to account for it, and I did not try to account for it or to find out whether there was any reason for the fear. I just felt 'I am going to die' and began thinking what to do about it. It did not occur to me to consult a doctor or my elders or friends; I felt that I had to solve the problem myself, there and then.

"The shock of the fear of death drove my mind inwards and I said to myself mentally, without actually framing the words: 'Now death has come; what does it mean? What is it that is dying? This body dies.' And I at once dramatised the occurrence of death. I lay with my limbs stretched out stiff as though *rigor mortis* had set in and imitated a corpse so as to give greater reality to the enquiry. I held my breath and kept my lips tightly closed so that no sound could escape, so that neither the word 'I' nor any other word could be uttered. 'Well then,' I said to myself, 'this body is dead. It will be carried stiff to the burning ground and there burnt and reduced to ashes. But with the death of this body am I dead? Is the body 'I'? It is silent and inert but I feel the full force of my personality and even the voice of the 'I' within me, apart from it. So I am Spirit transcending the body. The body dies but the Spirit that transcends it cannot be touched by death. That means I am the deathless Spirit.' All this was not dull thought; it flashed through me vividly as living truth which I perceived directly, almost without thought-process. 'I' was something very real, the only real thing about my present state, and all the conscious activity connected with my body was centred on that 'I'. From that moment onwards the 'I' or Self focused attention on itself by a powerful fascination. Fear of death had vanished once and for all. Absorption in the Self continued unbroken from that time on. Other thoughts might come and go like the various notes of music, but the 'I' continued like the fundamental *sruti* note that underlies and blends with all the other notes.[1] Whether the body was engaged in talking, reading or anything else, I was still centred on 'I'. Previous to that crisis I had no clear perception of my Self and was not consciously attracted to it. I felt no perceptible or direct interest in it, much less any inclination to dwell permanently in it."

Thus simply described, without pretension or verbiage, the state attained might seem no different from egotism, but that is due only to the ambiguity in the words 'I' and 'Self'. The difference is brought out by the attitude towards death, for one whose interest is centred in the ego, the 'I' as a separate individual being, has a dread of death which threatens the dissolution of the ego, whereas here the fear of death had vanished forever in the realization that the 'I' was one with the universal deathless Self which is the Spirit and the Self of every man. Even to say that he knew he was One with the Spirit is inadequate, since it suggests a separate 'I' who knew this, whereas the 'I' in him was itself consciously the Spirit.

---

[1] The monotone persisting through a Hindu piece of music, like the thread on which beads are strung, represents the Self persisting through all the forms of being.

Years later the difference was expounded by Sri Bhagavan to Paul Brunton, a Western seeker.[1]

BRUNTON: What exactly is this Self of which you speak? If what you say is true there must be another self in man.

SRI RAMANA: Can a man be possessed of two identities, two selves? To understand this matter it is first necessary for a man to analyse himself. Because it has long been his habit to think as others think, he has never faced his 'I' in the true manner. He has not a correct picture of himself; he has too long identified himself with the body and the brain. Therefore I tell you to pursue this enquiry, 'Who am I?'

You ask me to describe this true Self to you. What can be said? It is That out of which the sense of the personal 'I' arises and into which it will have to disappear.

BRUNTON: Disappear? How can one lose the feeling of one's personality?

SRI RAMANA: The first and foremost of all thoughts, the primeval thought in the mind of every man, is the thought 'I'. It is only after the birth of this thought that any other thoughts can arise at all. It is only after the first personal pronoun, 'I', has arisen in the mind that the second

---

[1] This and the other quotations from Paul Brunton given in this book are based on his *A Search in Secret India*, published by Rider & Co., London, and reproduced by the Ashram with his permission.

personal pronoun, 'you', can make its appearance. If you could mentally follow the 'I' thread until it led you back to its source you would discover that, just as it is the first thought to appear, so it is the last to disappear. This is a matter which can be experienced.

BRUNTON: You mean that it is possible to conduct such a mental investigation into oneself?

SRI RAMANA: Certainly. It is possible to go inwards until the last thought, 'I', gradually vanishes.

BRUNTON: What is then left? Will a man then become quite unconscious or will he become an idiot?

SRI RAMANA: No; on the contrary, he will attain that consciousness which is immortal and he will become truly wise when he has awakened to his true Self, which is the real nature of man.

BRUNTON: But surely the sense of 'I' must also pertain to that?

SRI RAMANA: The sense of 'I' pertains to the person, the body and brain. When a man knows his true Self for the first time something else arises from the depths of his being and takes possession of him. That something is behind the mind; it is infinite, divine, eternal. Some people call it the Kingdom of Heaven, others call it the soul and others again Nirvana, and Hindus call it Liberation; you may give it what name you wish. When this happens a man has not really lost himself; rather he has found himself.

Unless and until a man embarks on this quest of the true Self, doubt and uncertainty will follow his footsteps through life. The greatest kings and statesmen try to rule others when in their heart of hearts they know that they cannot rule themselves. Yet the greatest power is at the command of the man who has penetrated to his inmost depth. . . . What is the use of knowing about everything else when you do not yet know who you are? Men avoid this enquiry into the true Self, but what else is there so worthy to be undertaken?

This whole *sadhana* took barely half an hour, and yet it is of the utmost importance to us that it *was* a *sadhana*, a striving towards light, and not an effortless awakening; for a Guru normally guides his disciples along the path that he himself has trod. That Sri Bhagavan completed within half an hour not merely the *sadhana* of a lifetime but, for most *sadhakas*, of many lifetimes, does not alter the fact that it was a striving by Self-enquiry such as he later enjoined on his followers. He warned them that the consummation towards which it leads is not normally attained quickly but only after long striving, but he also said that it is "the one infallible means, the only direct one, to realize the unconditioned, absolute Being that you really are" (*Maharshi's Gospel*, Part II). He said that it immediately sets up the process of transmutation, even though it may be long before this is completed. "But the moment the ego-self tries to know itself it begins to partake less and less of the body in which it is immersed and more and more of the consciousness of Self."

It is also significant that, although knowing nothing of the theory or practice of *sadhana*, Sri Bhagavan did in fact use *pranayama* or breath-control as an aid to concentration. So also he did admit of it as a legitimate help towards attaining thought-control, although he discouraged its use except for that purpose and never actually enjoined it.

"Breath-control is also a help. It is one of the various methods that are intended to help us attain one-pointedness. Breath-control can also help to control the wandering mind and attain this one-pointedness and therefore it can be used. But one should not stop there. After obtaining control of the mind through breathing exercises one should not rest content with any experience that may accrue therefrom, but should harness the controlled mind to the question 'Who am I?' till the mind merges in the Self."

This changed mode of consciousness naturally produced a change in Venkataraman's sense of values and habits of life. Things that had formerly been valued lost all attraction, conventional aims in life became unreal, what had been ignored exercised a strong compulsion. The adaptation of life to this new state of awareness cannot have been easy in one who was still a schoolboy and who lacked all theoretical training in spiritual life. He spoke to no one about it and for the time being remained in the family and continued to go to school; in fact he made as little outer change as possible. Nevertheless, it was inevitable that his family should notice his changed behaviour and resent some features of it. This also he has described.

"The consequences of this new awareness were soon noticed in my life. In the first place, I lost what little interest I had in my outer relationship with friends and relatives and went through my studies mechanically. I would hold an open book in front of me to satisfy my relatives that I was reading, when in reality my attention was far away from any such superficial matter. In my dealings with people I became meek and submissive. Formerly if I was given more work than other boys I might complain, and if any boy annoyed me I would retaliate. None of them would dare make fun of me or take liberties with me. Now all that was changed. Whatever work was given, whatever teasing or annoyance there was, I would put up with it quietly. The former ego that resented and retaliated had disappeared. I stopped going out with friends to play games and preferred solitude. I would often sit alone, especially in a posture suitable for meditation, and become absorbed in the Self, the Spirit, the force or current which constituted me. I would continue in this despite the jeers of my elder brother who would sarcastically call me 'sage' or 'yogi' and advise me to retire into the jungle like the ancient Rishis.

"Another change was that I no longer had any likes or dislikes with regard to food. Whatever was given to me, tasty or insipid, good or bad, I would swallow with like indifference.

"One of the features of my new state was my changed attitude to the Minakshi Temple.[1]

Formerly I used to go there very occasionally with friends to look at the images and put the sacred ash and vermilion on my brow and would return home almost unmoved. But after the Awakening I went there almost every evening. I used to go alone and stand motionless for a long time before an image of Siva or Minakshi or Nataraja and the sixty-three Saints, and as I stood there waves of emotion overwhelmed me. The soul had given up its hold on the

---

[1] The great temple at Madura.

body when it renounced the 'I-am-the-body' idea and it was seeking some fresh anchorage; hence the frequent visits to the temple and the outpouring of the soul in tears. This was God's play with the soul. I would stand before Iswara, the Controller of the universe and of the destinies of all, the Omniscient and Omnipresent, and sometimes pray for the descent of His Grace upon me so that my devotion might increase and become perpetual like that of the sixty-three Saints. More often I would not pray at all but silently allow the deep within to flow on and into the deep beyond. The tears that marked this overflow of the soul did not betoken any particular pleasure or pain. I was not a pessimist; I knew nothing of life and had not learnt that it was full of sorrow. I was not actuated by any desire to avoid rebirth or seek Liberation or even to obtain dispassion or salvation. I had read no books except the *Periapuranam*, the Bible and bits of Thayumanavar and *Thevaram*. My conception of Iswara[1] was similar to that found in the *Puranas*; I had never heard of Brahman,[2] *samsara*[3] and so forth. I did not yet know that there was an Essence or Impersonal Real underlying everything and that Iswara and I were both identical with it. Later, at Tiruvannamalai, as I listened to the *Ribhu Gita* and other sacred books, I learnt all this and found that the books were analysing and naming what I had felt intuitively without analysis or name. In the language of the books I should

---

[1] Iswara, the Supreme Being, corresponds to the Western conception of a Personal God.

[2] Brahman is the Impersonal Reality underlying Personal God, universe and man.

[3] *Samsara* is the succession of births and deaths terminated only by the Liberation of Self-realization.

describe the state I was in after the awakening as *Suddha Manas* or *Vijnana* or the intuition of the Illumined."

It was quite different from the state of the mystic who is transported into ecstasy for a brief unaccountable while, after which the gloomy walls of the mind close round him again. Sri Bhagavan was already in constant, unbroken awareness of the Self and he has said explicitly that there was no more *sadhana*, no more spiritual effort, after this. There was no more striving towards abidance in the Self because the ego, whose opposition it is that causes strife, had been dissolved and there was none left with whom to strive. Further progress towards continuous, fully conscious Identity with the Self, established in fully normal outer life and radiating Grace upon those who approached him, was henceforth natural and effortless; and yet that there was such progress is indicated by Sri Bhagavan's saying that the soul was still seeking a fresh anchorage. Things such as emulation of the Saints and concern as to what his elders would think still show a remnant of practical acceptance of duality which was later to disappear. There was also a physical sign of the continuing process. A constant burning sensation was felt in the body from the time of the Awakening until the moment when he entered the inner shrine of the temple at Tiruvannamalai.

3
THE JOURNEY

VENKATARAMAN'S changed mode of life caused friction. Schoolwork was more neglected than ever and, even though it was not now for games but for prayer and meditation, his uncle and elder brother became increasingly critical of what seemed to them an unpractical attitude. From their point of view, Venkataraman was simply the adolescent son of a middle class family who should pull his weight and equip himself to earn money and help the others.

The crisis came on August 29th, some two months after the Awakening. Venkataraman had been given an exercise in Bain's English Grammar to copy out three times for not learning it. It was the forenoon and he was sitting upstairs in the same room with his elder brother. He had copied it out twice and was about to do so for the third time when the futility of it struck him so forcibly that he pushed the papers away and, sitting cross-legged, abandoned himself to meditation.[1]

Annoyed at the sight, Nagaswami remarked caustically, "What use is all this to such a one?" The meaning was obvious: that one who wished to live like a sadhu had no right to enjoy the amenities of home life. Venkataraman recognised the truth of the remark and, with that ruthless acceptance of truth (or justice, which is applied truth) that characterised him, he rose to his feet to leave the house there and then and go forth, renouncing everything. For him that meant Tiruvannamalai and the holy hill, Arunachala.

However, he knew that it was necessary to use guile, because authority is very strong in a Hindu household and his uncle and brother would not let him go if they knew. So he said he had to go back to school to attend a special class on electricity.

Unconsciously providing him with funds for the journey, his brother said, "Then take five rupees from the box downstairs and pay my college fees on the way."

It was no spiritual blindness in Venkataraman's family that prevented them from recognising his attainment. Nobody did. The glory, the power, the divinity of his state was still concealed. A school friend, Ranga Aiyar, visiting him some years later at Tiruvannamalai, was so struck with awe that he fell prostrate at

---

[1] The word 'meditation' may be misleading as this normally implies thought and reflection. Its use by Sri Bhagavan has already been remarked upon. It may be added here that he used it for *samadhi*, for which there is no exact English equivalent but which means rather thought-free contemplation or immersion in the Spirit. He also used it to mean the effort to attain *samadhi* by Self-enquiry, which is not so much thought as the shutting off of thought.

his feet, but now he also saw only the Venkataraman he knew.
He asked later why this was and Sri Bhagavan replied merely
that none of them perceived the change.

Ranga Aiyar also asked, "Why did you not tell at least me
that you were leaving home?"

And he replied: "How could I? I myself did not know."

Venkataraman's aunt was downstairs. She gave him the five
rupees and served him a meal, which he ate hastily. There was an
atlas there and he opened it and found that the nearest station it
gave to Tiruvannamalai was at Tindivanam. Actually, a branch
line had already been constructed to Tiruvannamalai, but the atlas
was an old one and did not show it. Estimating that three rupees
would be enough for the journey, he took only so much. He
wrote a letter to his brother to allay anxiety and discourage pursuit
and left the remaining two rupees with it. The letter ran:

> "I have set out in quest of my Father in accordance
> with his command. It is on a virtuous enterprise that this
> has embarked, therefore let none grieve over this act and
> let no money be spent in search of this. Your college fees
> have not been paid. Two rupees are enclosed herewith."

This whole incident illustrates Sri Bhagavan's saying that
his soul, loosened from its anchorage to the body, was still seeking
permanent anchorage in the Self with which he had realized his
Oneness. The subterfuge about the electricity class, harmless
though it was, would not have been possible later. Neither would
the idea of a quest, for he who has found does not seek. When
devotees fell at his feet he was One with the Father and no
longer in search of the Father. The letter itself illustrates the
transition from the love and devotion of duality to the blissful
serenity of Oneness. It begins with the duality of 'I' and 'my

Father' and the statement of a command and a quest; but then in the second sentence it no longer refers to its writer as 'I' but as 'this'. And at the end when the time came to sign, he realized that there was no ego and therefore no name to sign and ended with a dash in place of a signature. Never again did he write a letter and never again did he sign a name, though he twice wrote what his name had been. Once also, years later, a Chinese visitor to the Ashram was given a copy of Sri Bhagavan's book *Who Am I?* and, in the courteous but persistent way of the Chinese, pressed Sri Bhagavan to sign it. Sri Bhagavan finally took it and wrote in it the Sanskrit symbol for OM, the sacred monosyllable representing the Primordial Sound underlying all creation.

Venkataraman took three rupees and left the remaining two. It is significant that he took no more than was necessary for the journey to Tiruvannamalai.

It was about noon when he left home. The station was half a mile away and he walked fast because the train was due to leave at twelve. However, late though he was, the train had not yet arrived when he reached the station. There was a table of fares and he looked up the third-class fare to Tindivanam and found it to be two rupees and thirteen annas. He bought a ticket, leaving himself three annas change. Had he looked a few lines lower down he would have seen the name Tiruvannamalai and that the fare to it was exactly three rupees. The events of the journey are symbolical of the arduous journey an aspirant (*sadhaka*) makes to his goal: first there was the favour of Providence in granting the money and allowing the train to be caught, although he started out late; then the provision made was exactly what was needed to reach the destination but the heedlessness of the traveller lengthened the journey and caused hardships and adventures on the way.

Venkataraman sat silent among the passengers, lost in the exultation of his quest. Several stations passed thus. A white-bearded *Maulvi*[1] who had been enlarging on the lives and teachings of the Saints turned to him:

"And where are you going, Swami?"

"To Tiruvannamalai."

"So am I," replied the Maulvi.

"What! To Tiruvannamalai?"

"Not exactly but to the next station."

"What is the next station?"

"Tirukoilur."

Then, suspecting his mistake, Venkataraman exclaimed in surprise: "What! You mean the train goes to Tiruvannamalai?"

"A strange passenger, you!" rejoined the Maulvi. "And where did you buy a ticket to?"

"To Tindivanam."

"Oh dear! There is no need to go so far at all. We get out at Villupuram Junction and change there for Tiruvannamalai and Tirukoilur."

Providence having given him the needed information, Venkataraman sank once more into the bliss of *samadhi* (absorption). By sunset the train had reached Trichinopoly (now called Tiruchirapalli) and he began to feel hungry, so he spent half an anna on two country pears, that is the huge, woody variety that grow in the hills of South India. To his surprise his appetite was sated almost at the first bite though up till then he had always eaten heartily. He continued in a blissful state of waking sleep until the train reached Villupuram at three o'clock in the morning.

---

[1] Muslim pandit or theologian.

He remained at the station till daybreak and then wandered out into the town to look for the road to Tiruvannamalai, deciding to walk the rest of the way. However, the name was not to be found on any signpost and he did not like to ask. Feeling tired and hungry after walking about, he entered a hotel and asked for food. The hotel-keeper told him the meal would be ready only at noon so he sat down to wait and immediately lapsed into meditation. The meal came and, after eating it, he proffered two annas in payment, but the hotel-keeper must have been struck by this fine-looking Brahmin youth with long hair and gold earrings sitting there like a sadhu. He asked how much money Venkataraman had and, on hearing that he had only two and a half annas all told, refused to accept payment. He also explained that Mambalapattu, a name that Venkataraman had seen on a signpost, was on the way to Tiruvannamalai. Venkataraman thereupon returned to the station and bought a ticket to Mambalapattu, which was as far as his remaining annas would take him.

He reached Mambalapattu in the afternoon and from there set out to walk. By nightfall he had gone ten miles. Before him was the temple of Arayaninallur built on a large rock. The long walk, most of it in the heat of the day, had tired him and he sat down by the temple to rest. Shortly after, someone came along and opened it for the temple priest and others to make puja. Venkataraman entered and sat down in the pillared hall, the only part that was not yet quite dark. He immediately beheld a brilliant light pervading the whole temple. Thinking it must be an emanation from the image of the God in the inner sanctuary, he went to look but found that it was not. Nor was it any physical light. It disappeared and he sat down again in meditation.

He was soon disturbed by the cook calling out that it was time to lock up the temple as the puja was finished. Thereupon he approached the priest and asked if they had anything for him to eat but was told there was nothing. He then asked to be allowed to stay there till morning but that was also refused. The *pujaris* (worshippers) said they were going to Kilur, about three-quarters of a mile away, to perform puja at the temple there as well and that after that he might get something to eat, so he accompanied them. As soon as they entered the temple he was again plunged in the blissful absorption called *samadhi*. It was nine o'clock by the time the puja was finished and they sat down to supper. Again Venkataraman asked. It seemed at first that there would be nothing for him, but the temple drummer had been impressed by his appearance and devout manner and gave him his share. He wanted water to drink with it and, holding his leaf-plate with rice, was shown the way to the house of a *sastri* (pandit) nearby who would give him water. While standing in front of the house, waiting for it, he stumbled on a few paces and then collapsed in sleep or faint. A few minutes later he came round to find a small crowd looking on curiously. He drank the water, gathered up and ate some of the rice he had spilled, and then lay down on the ground and slept.

Next morning, Monday, August 31st, was Gokulashtami, the birth anniversary of Sri Krishna and one of the most auspicious days in the Hindu calendar. Tiruvannamalai was still twenty miles distant. Venkataraman walked about for some time looking for the road to it and again began to feel tired and hungry. Like most Brahmins at a time when ancient customs still held more sway than they do today, he wore gold earrings, and in his case they were set with rubies. He took them off in order to raise money on them and finish the journey by train, but the

question was, where and with whom? He stopped at random at
a house which turned out to belong to one Muthukrishna
Bhagavatar and asked for food. The housewife must have been
deeply impressed by the appearance at her door of a Brahmin
youth of beautiful countenance and shining eyes on the day of
Krishna's birth; she gave him a large cold meal and although, as
in the train two days ago, his appetite disappeared after the first
mouthful, she stood over him in true motherly fashion and made
him finish it.

There remained the question of the earrings. They must
be worth some twenty rupees but he only wanted a loan of
four on them to cover any more expenses he might have on
his way. To avoid arousing suspicion he gave the pretext that
he was on a pilgrimage and his luggage had got lost, leaving
him destitute. Muthukrishna Bhagavatar examined the earrings
and, judging them to be genuine, advanced the four rupees.
However, he insisted on taking the youth's address and giving
his own so that they could be redeemed at any time. The good
couple kept him with them till noon and then gave him lunch
and packed up for him a parcel of sweets that had been prepared
for puja to Sri Krishna but not yet offered.

As soon as he left the house he tore up the address,
having no intention of ever redeeming the earrings. Finding
that there was no train to Tiruvannamalai till next morning,
he slept the night at the station. No man can end his journey
till the allotted time. It was the morning of September 1st,
1896, three days after leaving home, when he arrived at
Tiruvannamalai station.

With quick steps, his heart throbbing with joy, he hastened
straight to the great Temple. In mute sign of welcome, the gates
of the three high compound walls and all the doors, even that of

the inner shrine, stood open. There was no one else inside, so he entered the inner shrine alone and stood overcome before his Father Arunachaleswar.[1] There, in the bliss of Union, was the quest achieved and the journey ended.

---

[1] Iswara manifested as Arunachala.

4
SEEMING TAPAS

LEAVING THE TEMPLE, Venkataraman wandered out
into the town. Someone called out to ask whether he
wanted his tuft removed.[1] The question must have been
inspired, for there was no outer sign that this Brahmin youth
had renounced or intended to renounce the world. He
immediately consented and was conducted to the Ayyankulam
Tank where a number of barbers plied their trade. There he
had his head completely shaved. Then, standing on the steps
of the tank, he threw away his remaining money — a little
over three rupees. He never handled money again. He also

---

[1] An orthodox caste-Hindu wears a small tuft of hair at the back of his head;
removing it and shaving the head is a sign of renunciation.

threw away the packet of sweets which he was still holding. "Why give sweets to this block of a body?"

He took off the sacred thread that is a sign of caste and threw it away, for he who renounces the world renounces not only home and property but caste also and all civil status.

Then he took off the *dhoti*[1] he was wearing, tore off a strip to serve him as a loincloth, and threw the rest away.

So he returned to the temple, having completed the acts of renunciation. As he approached it he recollected that the Scriptures enjoin a bath after having one's hair cut, but he said to himself, "Why give this block of a body the luxury of a bath?" Immediately there was a short, sharp shower so that before entering the temple he had his bath.

He did not re-enter the inner shrine. There was no need. Indeed, it was three years before he went there again. He took up his abode in the thousand-pillared hall, a raised stone platform, open on all sides, the roof supported by a forest of slender, sculptured pillars, and there sat immersed in the Bliss of Being. Day after day, day and night, he sat unmoving. He no longer needed the world; its shadow existence had no interest for him as he sat absorbed in the Real. For some weeks he continued so, scarcely moving, never speaking.

So began the second phase of his life after Self-realization. During the first, the glory had been concealed and he had accepted the same conditions of life as previously, with the same obedience to teachers and elders; during the second he was turned inwards, completely ignoring the outer world; and this, as will be shown, merged gradually into the third, lasting for half a century, during which his radiance shone like the midday sun

---

[1] A white cloth wound round the body from the waist down.

on all who approached him. However, these phases applied only to the outer manifestation of his state: he declared explicitly and a number of times that there was absolutely no change or development in his state of consciousness or spiritual experience.

A sadhu known as Seshadri Swami, who had arrived at Tiruvannamalai a few years previously, took it on himself to look after the Brahmana Swami, as Venkataraman began to be called, so far as any looking after was needed. This was not altogether an advantage, because Seshadri Swami made the impression of being slightly deranged and thereby drew on himself the persecution of schoolboys. They now extended their attentions to his protégé whom they called 'Little Seshadri'. They began throwing stones at him, partly out of boyish cruelty, partly because they were intrigued to see one not much older than themselves sitting like a statue and, as one of them put it later, wanted to find out whether he was real or not.

Seshadri Swami's attempts to keep them off were not very successful; they sometimes had the opposite effect. So the Brahmana Swami sought refuge in the Patala Lingam, an underground vault in the thousand-pillared hall, dark and dank, where the sun's rays never penetrate. It was seldom that any human being entered; only ants, vermin and mosquitoes flourished there. They preyed upon him until his thighs were covered with sores that ran blood and pus. To the end of his life the marks remained. The few weeks he spent there were a descent into hell, and yet, absorbed in the Bliss of Being, he was unmoved by the torment; it was unreal to him. A pious woman, Ratnammal, entered the vault to take him food and besought him to leave the place and come to her house, but he made no sign of having heard. She left a clean cloth, begging him to sit or lie on it or use it against the insect pests, but he did not touch it.

Afraid to enter the dark vault, the youthful tormentors threw
stones at its entrance or broken pots that crashed and sent splinters
flying. Seshadri Swami mounted guard but this only incited them
the more. At noon one day a certain Venkatachala Mudali
approached the thousand-pillared hall and, indignant at seeing
boys throwing stones in the temple precincts, seized a stick and
drove them away. On coming back he saw Seshadri Swami
emerging from the gloomy recesses of the hall. He was startled
for a moment but quickly recovered and asked Seshadri Swami
whether he was hurt. "No," he replied, "but go and look at the
little Swami in there," and saying this he went away.

Astonished, Mudali descended the steps into the vault.
Coming from the bright daylight to the dark, he could see
nothing at first; gradually, however, his eyes grew accustomed
and he made out the form of the young Swami. Aghast at what
he saw, he went and told a sadhu who was working in the nearby
flower garden with a few disciples. They also came to look. The
young Swami neither moved nor spoke and seemed oblivious
of their presence, so they lifted him up bodily and carried him
out. They set him down before a shrine of Lord Subramania
without his showing any consciousness of what was happening.[1]

For about two months the Brahmana Swami stayed at the
Lord Subramania shrine. He would sit motionless in *samadhi*
(absorption) and sometimes nourishment had to be put into
his mouth as he paid no heed when it was offered him. For
some weeks he did not even trouble to tie on a loincloth. He
was looked after by a Mouni Swami (one who observes silence)
who also lived at the shrine.

---

[1] The Patala Lingam has been renovated in view of the sanctity it has acquired as the scene of *tapas* of Sri Bhagavan. It is well kept now and lit with
electric light, and portraits of Sri Bhagavan have been installed.

The shrine of the Goddess Uma in the temple was daily washed down with a mixture of milk, water, turmeric powder, sugar, bananas and other ingredients, and the Mouni used to take a tumbler of this strange concoction to the young Swami daily. He gulped it down, indifferent to the flavour, and it was all the nourishment he received. After sometime the temple priest noticed this and gave orders that pure milk should be supplied to the Mouni henceforth to be given to the Brahmana Swami.

After a few weeks the Brahmana Swami moved out to the temple garden, full of tall oleander bushes, some of them ten or twelve feet high. Here also he would sit immersed in bliss (*samadhi*). He even moved about in trance, for on waking to the world he would sometimes find himself under a different bush with no recollection of how he got there. He went next to the hall of the temple vehicles on which the images are taken in procession on holy days. Here also he would sometimes wake to the world to find his body in a different place, having avoided the various obstacles on the way without injury, though unaware.

After this he sat for sometime under a tree alongside the road that runs round the temple precincts within its outer wall and is used for temple processions. He remained for sometime here and at the Mangai Pillayar shrine. Annually large crowds of pilgrims throng to Tiruvannamalai for the festival of Kartikai, falling in November or December, when a beacon is lit on the summit of Arunachala in token of Siva's appearance as a pillar of light described in Chapter Six, and this year many came to gaze on the young Swami or prostrate themselves before him. It was at this time that the first regular devotee became attached to him. Uddandi Nayinar had engaged in spiritual studies but had not found peace therefrom. Seeing the young Swami immersed in perpetual *samadhi* and apparently oblivious of the body, he felt that here was realization and that through him he would find peace. It made him happy to serve the Swami but there was little he could do. He kept away the crowds of sightseers and stopped the persecution by the boys. Much of his time he spent reciting Tamil works expounding the supreme doctrine of Advaita (Non-duality). His great hope was to receive *upadesa*, spiritual instruction, from the Swami, but the Swami never spoke to him and he himself did not presume to speak first and intrude on his silence.

About this time, one Annamalai Tambiran passed by the young Swami's tree. He was so impressed by his serene beauty as he sat there in solitude, untouched by care and thought, that he fell on his face before him and thereafter went daily to bow down to him. He was a sadhu who used to walk through the town with a few companions, singing devotional songs. With the alms received he fed the poor and made puja at the tomb of his Adhina Guru (the founder of the line of his Gurus) outside the town.

After sometime it occurred to him that the young Swami would be less disturbed at Gurumurtam, as this shrine had come to be called, and also, as it was now the cool season, would be more sheltered. He hesitated to suggest it and talked the matter over first with Nayinar, since neither of them had ever spoken to the Swami. Finally he mustered up courage to make the suggestion. The Swami consented and in February 1897, less than half a year after his arrival at Tiruvannamalai, went with him to Gurumurtam.

There was no change in his mode of life when he arrived there. The floor of the shrine was infested with ants but the Swami seemed oblivious to their crawling over him and biting. After some time a stool was placed in one corner for him to sit on and its legs immersed in water to keep them away, but even then he leaned back against the wall and so made a bridge for them. From constant sitting there his back made a permanent imprint on the wall.

Pilgrims and sightseers began to throng to Gurumurtam and many would prostrate themselves before the Swami, some with prayers for boons and some out of pure reverence. The crowd became such that it was necessary to erect a bamboo palisade round his seat so as to prevent them at least from touching him.

At first Tambiran supplied the little food that was necessary out of that offered at the shrine of his Guru, but before long he left Tiruvannamalai. He told Nayinar that he would be back in a week but as things turned out he was away for more than a year. A few weeks later Nayinar also had to leave to go to his *math* (private temple or shrine) and the Swami was left without an attendant. There was no difficulty over food — in fact there were several devotees by now who wished to supply food regularly. The more pressing need was to keep away the crowds of sightseers and visitors.

It was not long before another regular attendant came. A Malayali sadhu named Palaniswami was devoting his life to the worship of God Vinayaka. He lived in great austerity, eating only one meal a day and that merely the food that had been offered to the God in puja, without even salt for seasoning. A friend of his, Srinivasa Iyer by name, said to him one day: "Why do you spend your life with this stone Swami? There is a young Swami in flesh and blood at Gurumurtam. He is steeped in *tapas* (austerity) like the young Dhruva in the Puranas. If you go and serve him and attach yourself to him your life will attain its purpose."

About the same time others also told him about the young Swami and that he had no attendant and what a blessing it would be to serve him. Accordingly he went to Gurumurtam to see. He was stirred to the depths at the very sight of the Swami. For sometime longer he continued his worship at the Vinayaka temple out of a sense of duty, but his heart was with the living Swami and before long his devotion to him became all absorbing. He consecrated the rest of his life to his service, remaining his attendant for twenty-one years.

There was little enough that he could do. He received food offerings from the devotees but all that the Swami would accept was a single cup of food at noon each day, the remainder being returned to the givers as *prasadam* (Grace in form of a gift). If he needed to go into town for any purpose — usually to get some spiritual or devotional book from a friend — he would lock up the shrine and on his return would find the Swami in the same position as he left him.

The Swami's body was utterly neglected. He ignored it completely. It was unwashed; his hair had grown again and was thick and matted; his finger-nails had grown long and curled over. Some took this to be a sign of great age and whispered that he had preserved his youth of body by yogic powers. Actually, his body was weakened to the limits of endurance. When he needed to go out he had barely the strength to rise. He would raise himself up a few inches and then sink back again, weak and dizzy, and would have to try several times before he could rise to his feet. On one such occasion he reached the door and was holding on to it with both hands when he perceived that Palaniswami was supporting him. Always averse to receiving help, he asked, "Why are you holding me?" and Palaniswami replied: "Swami was going to fall and I supported him to prevent him falling."

One who has attained Union with the Divine is sometimes worshipped in the same manner as a temple idol, with burning camphor, sandal-paste, flowers, libation and chanting. When Tambiran was at Gurumurtam he decided to worship the Swami in this way. The first day, the Swami was taken by surprise and he succeeded in his purpose, but the next day when Tambiran brought in his daily cup of food he saw written on the wall above the Swami with charcoal the words, in Tamil, "This is service enough for this," meaning that food was all that should be offered to this body.

It came as a surprise to his devotees that the Swami had mundane education and could read and write. One of them decided to utilise the fact to find out where he came from and what his name had been. He was an elderly man, Venkatarama Iyer by name, head accountant at the Taluq Office in town. He used to come every morning and sit for a while in meditation in the presence of the Swami before going to his work. A vow of silence is respected and from his not speaking it was presumed that the Swami had taken such a vow, but one who does not speak occasionally writes messages, and now that he knew the Swami could write, Venkatarama Iyer was insistent. He placed before him a sheet of paper and a pencil on one of the books that Palaniswami had brought there and besought him to write his name and place of origin.

The Swami made no response to his pleading until at last he declared that he would neither eat nor go to his office until he received the information he desired. Then he wrote in English, 'Venkataraman, Tiruchuzhi'. His knowing English came as a further surprise, but Venkatarama Iyer was puzzled by the name 'Tiruchuzhi' in English transliteration, especially by the 'zh'.

The Swami therefore took the book on which the paper had rested to see whether it was in Tamil so that he could point out the letter that is commonly transliterated as 'zh', a letter midway between 'r' and 'l' in sound. Finding it to be the *Periapuranam*, the book which had had so profound an effect on him before the spiritual awakening, he looked up the passage where Tiruchuzhi is mentioned as a town honoured in song by Sundaramurti Swami and showed it to Venkatarama Iyer.

In May 1898, after a little more than a year at Gurumurtam, the Swami moved to a neighbouring mango orchard. Its owner, Venkatarama Naicker, proposed the change to Palaniswami as the orchard could be locked and would afford more privacy. The Swami and Palaniswami each occupied a watchman's shelter there, and the owner gave the gardener strict instructions that nobody was to be admitted without Palaniswami's permission.

He stayed here about six months and it was here that he began to accumulate the vast erudition he later possessed. Characteristically, it was not from any desire for learning but purely to help a devotee. Palaniswami used to bring works of spiritual philosophy to study but the only ones he had access to were in Tamil, a language of which he knew very little, so that it caused him immense labour. Seeing him struggling in this way, the Swami picked up the books, read them through and gave him a brief synopsis of their essential teaching. His prior spiritual experience enabled him to understand at a glance what was expounded and his wonderful memory retained it when read, so that he became erudite almost without effort. In the same way, he later picked up Sanskrit, Telugu and Malayalam by reading books brought to him in these languages and answering questions in them.

5
THE QUESTION OF RETURN

WHEN THE YOUNG Venkataraman left home it came as a complete surprise to his family. Despite his changed manner and despite the family destiny, no one had anticipated it. Searches and enquiries were made without avail. His mother, who was staying at the time with relatives at Manamadura, was more distressed than any of them. She implored her brothers-in-law, Subbier and Nelliappier, to go out and search until they found him. A rumour was heard that he had joined a theatrical troupe playing traditional religious dramas in Trivandrum. Nelliappier promptly went there and made enquiries among the various dramatic companies, but of course without result. Still Alagammal refused to accept the failure and insisted on his going a second time and taking her with him. At Trivandrum she did in fact see a youth of Venkataraman's age and height and with similar hair who turned his back on her and went away. Feeling convinced that it was her Venkataraman and that he was avoiding her, she returned home dejected.

Subbier, the uncle with whom Venkataraman had stayed in Madura, died in August 1898. Nelliappier and his family went to attend the funeral and it was there that they had their first news of the missing Venkataraman. A young man who was attending the ceremony told them that during a recent visit to a *math* (private temple) in Madura he heard one Annamalai Tambiran speaking with great reverence of a young Swami at Tiruvannamalai. Hearing that the Swami came from Tiruchuzhi, he had asked for more details and learnt that his name was Venkataraman. "It must be your Venkataraman and he is now a revered Swami," he concluded.

Nelliappier was a second-grade pleader practising at Manamadura. On hearing this news he at once set out for Tiruvannamalai with a friend to verify it. They found their way to the Swami but he was already staying in the mango orchard and its owner, Venkatarama Naicker, refused them entrance: "He is *mouni* (has taken a vow of silence); why go in and disturb him?" Even when they pleaded that they were relatives the most he would allow was to send in a note to him. Nelliappier wrote on a piece of paper that he had with him, "Nelliappier, pleader of Manamadura, wishes to see you."

The Swami showed already that keen perception of mundane affairs coupled with complete detachment from them, which was to characterise him later and which surprised so many devotees. He observed that the paper on which the note was written came from the Registration Department and had some office matter on the back of it in the handwriting of his elder brother, Nagaswami, from which he deduced that Nagaswami had become a clerk in the Registration Department. Just the same in later years, he would turn a letter over and examine its address and postmark before opening it.

He gave permission for the visitors to enter, but when they did so, sat aloof and silent without a trace of the interest he had just shown in examining the note. Any sign of interest would only have encouraged the vain hope of his return. Nelliappier was deeply moved to see him in this state — a Swami but unkempt, unwashed, with matted hair and long nails. Supposing him to be *mouni*, he addressed himself instead to Palaniswami and Naicker, explaining that it gave him great pleasure to find that one of his family had attained such a high state but that the creature comforts should not be ignored.

The Swami's relatives wished to have him near them. They would put no pressure on him to abandon his vows or mode of life; let him continue a *mouni* (silent) and an ascetic, but at Manamadura, near where Nelliappier lived, there was the shrine of a great saint, he could stay there and his wants would be attended to without disturbing him. The pleader pleaded with all his eloquence, but in this case without avail. The Swami sat motionless with no sign even of having heard. Nelliappier had no option but to accept his failure. He wrote to Alagammal the good news that her son had been found coupled with the distressing news that he was quite changed and would not go back to them. After five days at Tiruvannamalai, he returned to Manamadura.

Shortly after this the Swami left the mango orchard and went to a small temple of Arunagirinathar to the west of Ayyankulam tank. Always reluctant to depend on others for service, he decided now to go out daily and beg his food instead of letting Palaniswami provide for him. "You go one way to beg your food and I will go another," he bade him; "Let us not live together." To Palaniswami it was a terrible blow. Devotion to the Swami was his mode of worship. He went out alone as bidden but nightfall found him back at Arunagirinathar Temple. How could he live without his Swami? He was allowed to stay.

The Swami was still maintaining silence. He would stop at the threshold of a house and clap his hands and if any food was given him would receive it in his cupped hands and eat it standing in the road. Even though invited, he would never enter a house. He went on a different street each day and never begged twice from the same house. He said later that he had begged in nearly all the streets of Tiruvannamalai.

After a month at the Arunagirinathar Temple he took up his abode in one of the towers of the great temple and the *alari* garden in the temple. He was already followed by devotees wherever he went. He stayed here only a week and then went to Pavalakunru, one of the eastern spurs of Arunachala, and stayed in the temple there. He would sit here as before, immersed in *samadhi* (the Bliss of Being), and only leave the place to beg food while Palaniswami was away. It often happened that the temple priest would lock him in and go away after performing puja, not troubling to look and see whether he was inside.

It was here that Alagammal found her son. After receiving the news from Nelliappier, she waited until the Christmas holidays when her eldest son, Nagaswami, was free to accompany her and then went to Tiruvannamalai. She recognised her Venkataraman immediately, despite his wasted body and matted hair. With all a mother's love she lamented his condition and besought him to go back with her, but he sat unmoved, not answering, not even showing that he heard. Day after day she returned, bringing him tasty things to eat, entreating and reproaching, but without effect. One day, stung by his apparent lack of feeling for her, she burst into tears. He still did not answer but, lest his compassion should show and give her false hopes of what could not happen, he rose and walked away. Another day she enlisted the sympathy of the devotees who had gathered around, pouring out her grief to them and beseeching them to intervene. One of them, Pachaiyappa Pillai, said to the Swami: "Your mother is weeping and praying; why do you not at least give her an answer? Whether it is 'yes' or 'no' you can reply to her. Swami need not break his vow of silence. Here are pencil and paper; Swami can at least write what he has to say."

He took the pencil and paper and, in utterly impersonal language, wrote:

"The Ordainer controls the fate of souls in accordance with their *prarabdhakarma* (destiny to be worked out in this life, resulting from the balance sheet of actions in past lives). Whatever is destined not to happen will not happen, try as you may. Whatever is destined to happen will happen, do what you may to prevent it. This is certain. The best course, therefore, is to remain silent."

In essence, this is the same as Christ's saying to his mother: "Woman, what have I to do with you? Don't you know that I have to be about my Father's business?" In form it is very typical of Sri Bhagavan, first that he should stay silent when the answer could only be negative, and then that when the silence was not accepted and, under further pressure, he did give an answer, it was couched in such general terms as to be an impersonal doctrinal utterance and yet at the same time an answer to the specific question according to the needs of the questioner.

Sri Bhagavan was uncompromising in his teaching that whatever is to happen will happen, while at the same time he taught that whatever happens is due to *prarabdha*, a man's balance sheet of destiny acting according to so rigorous a law of cause and effect that even the word 'justice' seems too sentimental to express it. He refused ever to be entangled in a discussion on free will and predestination, for such theories, although contradictory on the mental plane, may both reflect aspects of truth. He would say "Find out who it is who is predestined or has free will."

He said explicitly: "All the actions that the body is to perform are already decided upon at the time it comes into existence: the only freedom you have is whether or not to identify yourself with the body." If one acts a part in a play, the whole part is written out beforehand and one acts as faithfully whether one is Caesar who is stabbed or Brutus who stabs, being unaffected by it because one knows one is not that person. In the same way, he who realizes his identity with the deathless Self acts his part on the human stage without fear or anxiety, hope or regret, not being touched by the part played. If one were to ask what reality one has when all one's actions are determined, it would lead only to the question: Who, then, am I? If the ego that thinks it makes decisions is not real and yet I know that I exist, what is the reality of me? This is only a preparatory, mental version of the quest that Sri Bhagavan prescribed, but it is an excellent preparation for the real quest.

And yet, the apparently conflicting view that a man makes his own destiny is no less true, since everything happens by the law of cause and effect and every thought, word and action brings about its repercussion. Sri Bhagavan was as definite about this as other Masters. He said to a devotee, Sivaprakasam Pillai, in a reply quoted in Chapter Ten, "As beings reap the fruit of their actions in accordance with God's laws, the responsibility is theirs, not His." He constantly stressed the need for effort. It is recorded in *Maharshi's Gospel* that a devotee complained: "After leaving this Ashram in October, I was aware of the Peace that prevails in Sri Bhagavan's presence enfolding me for about ten days. All the time, while busy in my work, there was an undercurrent of that peace in unity; it was almost like the dual consciousness which one experiences while half asleep at a dull lecture. Then it faded out entirely and the old stupidities came in instead." And Sri Bhagavan replied: "If you strengthen the mind that peace will become constant. Its duration is proportionate to the strength of mind acquired by repeated practice." In *Spiritual Instruction* a devotee referred explicitly to the apparent contradiction between destiny and effort: "If, as is said, everything happens according to destiny, even the obstacles that retard and prevent one from successfully carrying out the meditation may have to be considered insuperable, as being set up by such irrevocable destiny. How, then, can one ever hope to surmount them?" And to this Sri Bhagavan replied: "That which is called 'destiny', preventing meditation, exists only to the externalised and not to the introverted mind. Therefore he who seeks inwardly in quest of the Self, remaining as he is, does not get frightened by any impediment that may seem to stand in the way of carrying on his practice of meditation. The very thought of such obstacles is the greatest impediment."

The concluding statement in the message he wrote out — "The best course, therefore, is to remain silent" — applied specifically to his mother, since she was asking what could not be granted. It applies to people in general in the sense that "it is no use kicking against the pricks", opposing destiny that cannot be averted; but it does not mean that no effort should ever be made. The man who says, "Everything is predestined, therefore I will make no effort," is intruding the false assumption "and I know what is predestined" — it may be that he is cast in a part in which effort has to be made. As Sri Krishna told Arjuna in the *Bhagavad Gita*, his own nature will compel him to make effort.

The mother returned home and the Swami remained as before. And yet not quite. During the two and a quarter years that he spent in temples and shrines at Tiruvannamalai the first signs of a return to an outwardly normal life were already appearing. He had already begun to take food daily at a regular hour and then, so as not to be dependent on anyone, to go out in search of it. He had spoken a few times. He had begun to respond to devotees, to read books and to expound the essence of their teaching.

When he first came to Tiruvannamalai he sat immersed in the Bliss of Being, utterly ignoring the world and the body. He would take food only if it was brought to his hands or mouth and even then barely enough to sustain the body. This has been described as *tapas*, but the word *tapas* covers a very composite meaning. It implies concentration leading to austerity, normally in penance for past indulgence and to root out all desire for its repetition and restrain the outgoing energy which seeks a vehicle in the mind and senses. That is to say that *tapas* normally means striving for realization by means of penance and austerity. In the case of Sri Bhagavan the elements of strife, penance and forcible restraint were completely lacking, since the false identification of the 'I' with the body and the resultant attachment to the body had already been broken. There was even no austerity from his point of view, since he had utterly ceased to identify himself with the body that underwent austerity. He intimated this in later years by saying, "I did not eat, so they said I was fasting; I did not speak, so they said I was *mouni*." To put it quite simply, the seeming austerity was not in quest of Realization but as a result of Realization. He has explicitly said that there was no more *sadhana* (quest or striving) after the spiritual Awakening at his uncle's house at Madura.

So also, Sri Bhagavan was not a *mouni* in the usual sense of observing a vow of silence in order to shut himself off from contact with others. Having no worldly needs, he simply had no need to speak; moreover, he has explained that, on seeing a *mouni*, it occurred to him that not speaking would be a good defence against disturbance.

In the early months, immersion in Bliss often shut off perception of the manifested world. He has referred to this in his picturesque style:

"Sometimes I opened my eyes and it was morning, sometimes it was evening: I did not know when the sun rose or when it set." To some extent this continued, only it became rare instead of usual. In later years Sri Bhagavan once said that he often heard the beginning of the *parayanam* (chanting of the Vedas) and then the end, but had been so absorbed that he had heard nothing in between and wondered how they had got to the end so soon and whether they had left anything out. However, even during the early months at Tiruvannamalai, there was often full observance of events and in later years he would relate things that had happened at this period, of which people at the time thought he was unaware.

Complete absorption in the Self with resultant oblivion to the manifested world is termed *nirvikalpa samadhi*. This is a state of blissful trance but is not permanent. Sri Bhagavan has

compared it (in *Maharshi's Gospel*) to a bucket of water lowered
into a well. In the bucket is water (the mind) which is merged
with that in the well (the Self), but the rope and bucket (the
ego) still exist to draw it out again. The highest state, complete
and final, is *sahaja samadhi*, referred to briefly at the beginning
of Chapter Two. This is pure uninterrupted Consciousness,
transcending the mental and physical plane and yet with full
awareness of the manifested world and full use of the mental
and physical faculties, a state of perfect equilibrium, perfect
harmony, beyond even bliss. This he has compared with the
waters of a river merged in those of the ocean. In this state
the ego with all its limitations is dissolved once and for ever
in the Self. This is absolute freedom, pure consciousness, pure
I-am-ness no longer limited to the body or the individuality.

Sri Bhagavan was already in this supreme state although
the outer awareness was not yet continuous. The return to outer
activity that came later was only apparent and involved no real
change. As he explained in *Maharshi's Gospel*:

> "In the case of the *Jnani* (Enlightened) the rise or
> existence of the ego is only apparent and he enjoys his
> unbroken transcendental experience in spite of such
> apparent rise or existence of the ego, keeping his attention
> always on the Source. This ego is harmless; it is like the
> skeleton of a burnt rope — though it has a form it is no
> use to tie anything with."

6
ARUNACHALA

THERE IS A ruggedness about the scene. Boulders lie as though scattered by a giant hand. Dry thorn and cactus fences, sun-parched fields, small hills eroded into gaunt shapes; and yet huge shady trees along the dusty road, and here and there, near tank or well, the vivid green of paddy fields. And rising up out of this rough beauty the hill of Arunachala. Though only 2,682 feet high it dominates the countryside. From the south, the side of the Ashram, it is deceptively simple — just a symmetrical hill with two almost equal foothills, one on either side. To make the symmetry more perfect, it wears most mornings a crown of white cloud or haze about the summit. But it is astonishing how the aspect changes as one treads the eight-mile road around it, going the prescribed way, from south to west, with one's right side to the hill; and each aspect has its character and symbolism — that where it flings back an echo, that where the peak barely shows between two foothills, like the Self in the interval between two thoughts, that of the five peaks, that of Siva and Sakti, and others.

Sacred tanks mark the eight directions of space and *mantapams* (simple stone halls) stand at various significant points. Pre-eminent among these is the Dakshinamurti Mantapam at the southern point, for Dakshinamurti is Siva teaching in silence, and that is Arunachala.

"Who is the seer? When I sought within I watched the disappearance of the seer and what survived it. No thought of 'I saw' arose, so how could the thought 'I did not see' arise? Who has the power to convey this in words when even Thou couldst do so in ancient days by silence only (appearing as Dakshinamurti)? Only to convey by silence Thy State Thou standest as a Hill shining from heaven to earth."[1]

Sri Bhagavan always encouraged *pradakshina* (circuit) of the hill. Even in the case of the old or infirm he would not discourage it but only tell them to go slowly. Indeed, the *pradakshina* is supposed to be made slowly, "like a pregnant queen in her ninth month." Whether in silent meditation or with singing or blowing of conch, it is to be made on foot, not in any conveyance, and in fact barefoot. The most auspicious times are Sivarathri, the Night of Siva, and Kartikai, the day when the constellation of kartikai (pleiades) is in conjunction with the full moon, falling usually in November. On these occasions the continuous stream of devotees has been compared to a garland around the hill.

---

[1] *Eight Stanzas on Sri Arunachala* (*Arunachala Ashtakam*), v. 2, by Sri Bhagavan.

An elderly cripple was once hobbling on crutches along the road that skirts the hill. He had often done so in *pradakshina* but this time it was to leave Tiruvannamalai. He felt himself an encumbrance to his family; quarrels had broken out and he had decided to leave them and somehow make a living in a village. Suddenly a young Brahmin appeared before him and snatched away his crutches saying, "You don't deserve them." Before the anger that flushed him could find words he realized that his limbs were straight and he needed no crutches. He did not leave Tiruvannamalai; he stayed and was well known there. Sri Bhagavan told the story in all detail to some devotees and remarked on its similarity to that told in the *Arunachala Sthala Purana*. He was a young Swami on the hill at the time but he never said that it was he who appeared as the Brahmin youth.

Arunachala is one of the oldest and most sacred of all India's holy places. Sri Bhagavan declared that it is the heart of the earth, the spiritual centre of the world. Sri Shankara spoke of it as Mount Meru. The *Skanda Purana* declares: "That is the holy place. Of all, Arunachala is the most sacred. It is the heart of the world. Know it to be the secret and sacred Heart-centre of Siva." Many Saints have lived there, merging their sanctity with that of the hill. It is said, and confirmed by Sri Bhagavan, that to this day *Siddhas* (Sages with supernatural powers) dwell in its caves, whether with physical bodies or not, and some are said to have seen them as lights moving about the hill at night.

There is a *puranic* story about the origin of the hill. Once Vishnu and Brahma fell to disputing which of them was the greater. Their quarrelling brought chaos on earth, so the Devas approached Siva and besought him to settle the dispute. Siva thereupon manifested himself as a column of light from which a voice issued declaring that whoever could find its upper or lower end was the greater. Vishnu took the form of a boar and burrowed down into the earth to find the base, while Brahma took the form of a swan and soared upwards to seek its summit. Vishnu failed to reach the base of the column but "beginning to see within himself the Supreme Light which dwells in the hearts of all, he became lost in meditation, oblivious to the physical body and even unaware of himself, the one who sought." Brahma saw a screw pine flower falling through the air and, thinking to win by deception, returned with it and declared he had plucked it from the summit.

Vishnu admitted his failure and turned to the Lord in praise and prayer: "You are Self-knowledge. You are OM. You are the beginning and the middle and the end of everything. You are everything and illuminate everything." He was pronounced great while Brahma was abashed and confessed his fault.

In this legend Vishnu represents the ego or individuality and Brahma the mentality, while Siva is Atma, the Spirit.

The story continues that, because the lingam or column of light was too dazzling to behold, Siva manifested himself instead as the hill Arunachala, declaring: "As the moon derives its light from the sun, so other holy places shall derive their sanctity from Arunachala. This is the only place where I have taken this form for the benefit of those who wish to worship me and obtain illumination. Arunachala is OM itself. I will appear on the summit of this hill every year at Kartikai in the form of a peace-giving beacon." This refers not only to the sanctity of Arunachala itself but also to the pre-eminence of the doctrine of Advaita and the path of Self-enquiry of which Arunachala is the centre. One can understand this meaning in Sri Bhagavan's saying, "In the end everyone must come to Arunachala."

It was more than two years after his arrival at Tiruvannamalai before Sri Bhagavan began to live on the hill. Up till then he had stayed constantly at some shrine or temple. Only towards the close of 1898 did he take up his abode in the small temple at Pavalakunru, hallowed centuries ago by the presence of the great Saint Gautama Rishi, where his mother found him. He never left Arunachala again. Early next year he moved into a cave on the hill itself and thereafter he stayed in one cave or another until 1922 when he moved down to the foot of the hill. There the present Ashram grew up and there he spent his remaining years on earth.

While on the hill, he lived nearly all the time on the eastern slope. The Ashram stands at the south, just beside the Dakshinamurti *mantapam* (stone hall). 'The Southward-Facing' is one of the 108 Names of Bhagavan that are now chanted daily at his *samadhi* shrine. It is a name symbolical of spiritual authority in general, as the Sadguru is the Pole round which the world revolves, but it is in particular a name of Dakshinamurti. Dakshinamurti is Siva teaching in silence. In the verse quoted at the beginning of this chapter Sri Bhagavan identifies Arunachala with Dakshinamurti; in the following verse he speaks of Ramana and Arunachala as one:

> "In the recesses of the lotus-shaped heart of all, from Vishnu downwards, there shines as Absolute Consciousness, the *Paramatman* (Supreme Spirit) who is the same as Arunachala or Ramana. When the mind melts with love of him and reaches the inmost recess of the heart wherein he abides as the Beloved, the subtle eye of Absolute Consciousness opens and he reveals himself as pure Knowledge."

The cave to which Sri Bhagavan went first and in which he stayed longest is on the eastern slope. It is called Virupaksha after a Saint who dwelt and was buried there, probably in the sixteenth century. It is curiously shaped to resemble the sacred monosyllable OM, the tomb being in the inner recess, and it is said that the very sound OM can be heard within.

The trustees of the Virupaksha *math* (shrine) in town had also property rights over the cave and used to levy a small fee on pilgrims who visited it at the annual festival of Kartikai. At the time when Sri Bhagavan went there this practice had fallen into abeyance because two parties were disputing the ownership and a lawsuit was pending between them. When the case was decided the successful party resumed the levy, but by that time the stream of visitors had grown much larger and was continuous throughout the year, not merely at Kartikai; and since it was the presence of Sri Bhagavan that drew them there the fee had become, in effect, a tax on access to him. In order not to sanction this, he moved out of the cave to a level patch of ground in front of it and sat under the shade of a tree there. The agent thereupon shifted his place of collection to the outer perimeter to include access to the tree also. So Sri Bhagavan left and went to the Sadguruswami Cave lower down and then, after a short stay there, to another cave. The stream of visitors to Virupaksha Cave ceased, and the proprietors, finding that they had only inconvenienced the Swami without benefiting themselves, asked him to return and undertook not to levy the fee so long as he occupied the cave. On this condition he returned.

In the summer months Virupaksha Cave becomes oppressively hot. There is a cave near Mulaipal Tirtha tank near Virupaksha Cave, that is cooler and has a supply of pure water for drinking. A mango tree stands over it, giving shade, from which it has acquired the name of Mango Tree Cave. Two brothers, devotees of Sri Bhagavan, blasted away the overhanging rock and put up a front wall with a door and he occupied it during the hot months.

In the year 1900, shortly after Sri Bhagavan went to live on the hill, a devotee named Nalla Pillai from Kumbakonam came to Tiruvannamalai and took a photograph of him, the earliest portrait we have. It is the face of a beautiful youth, almost a child, yet with the strength and profundity of the Bhagavan.

During the early years on the hill Sri Bhagavan still maintained silence. His radiance had already drawn a group of devotees around him and an Ashram had come into being. It was not only seekers after Truth that were drawn to him but simple people, children, even animals. Young children from the town would climb the hill to Virupaksha Cave, sit near him, play around him, and go back feeling happy. Squirrels and monkeys would come up to him and eat out of his hand

He occasionally wrote out explanations or instructions for his disciples, but his not speaking did not really impede their training because, both now and later when he had resumed speech, his real teaching was through silence, in the tradition of Dakshinamurti, the tradition exemplified also in China by Lao Tsu and the early Taoist Sages. "That Tao which can be named is not the Tao" — the knowledge which can be formulated is not the true Knowledge. This silent teaching was a direct spiritual influence which the mind absorbed and later interpreted according to its ability. The first European visitor has thus described it:

"On reaching the cave we sat before him at his feet and said nothing. We sat thus for a long time and I felt lifted out of myself. For half an hour I looked into the Maharshi's eyes, which never changed their expression of deep contemplation. I began to realize somewhat that the body is the Temple of the Holy Ghost; I could feel only that his body was not the man: it was the instrument of God, merely a sitting, motionless corpse from which God was radiating terrifically. My own feelings were indescribable."[1]

Another, Paul Brunton, who arrived more a sceptic than a believer, has given the following account of the first impact the silence of Sri Bhagavan made upon his mind.

"It is an ancient theory of mine that one can take the inventory of a man's soul from his eyes. But before those of the Maharshi I hesitate, puzzled and baffled. . . .

"I cannot turn my gaze away from him. My initial bewilderment, my perplexity at being totally ignored, slowly fade away as this strange fascination begins to grip me more firmly. But it is not till the second hour of the uncommon scene that I become aware of a silent, resistless change which is taking place within my mind. One by one, the questions which I prepared in the train with such meticulous accuracy drop away. For it does not now seem to matter whether they are asked or not, and it does not matter whether I solve the problems which have hitherto troubled me. I know only that a steady river of quietness seems to be flowing near me, that a great peace is penetrating the inner reaches of my being, and that my thought-tortured brain is beginning to arrive at some rest."

---

[1] From a letter written to a friend in London by F. H. Humphreys and published by her in the *International Psychic Gazette*, London.

It was not only to the restless mind of the intellectual that the Grace of Bhagavan brought peace but to the grief-stricken heart also. Echammal, as she was called at the Ashram (her previous name had been Lakshmiammal), had been a happy wife and mother in the village of Mandakolathur, but before the age of twenty-five she lost first her husband, then her only son, then her only daughter. Stunned by her bereavement, tortured by memory, she could find no rest. She could no longer endure the place where she had been happy, the people among whom she had been happy. Thinking it might help her to forget, she travelled to Gokarnam in Bombay State to serve the holy men there, but she returned as grief-stricken as she went. Some friends told her of a young Swami at Tiruvannamalai who brought peace to those who sought. At once she set out. She had relatives in the town but did not go to them as the very sight of them would bring back her bitter memories. With a friend she climbed the hill to the Swami. She stood in silence before him, not telling her grief. There was no need. The compassion shining in his eyes was healing. A whole hour she stood, no word spoken, and then she turned and went down the hillside to the town, her steps light, the burden of her sorrow lifted.

Daily she visited the Swami thereafter. He was the sun that had dispersed her clouds. She could even recall her loved ones now without bitterness. She spent the rest of her life in Tiruvannamalai. She was able to take a small house there — her father left her a little money and her brothers helped her out — and many visiting devotees enjoyed her hospitality. She prepared food for Sri Bhagavan daily — which meant for the whole Ashram, because he would accept nothing that was not shared equally among all. Until age and failing health kept her away, she used to carry it up the hillside herself and would never eat until she had served them. As they grew in numbers her contribution came to be only a small addition to the general meal, but if ever she was delayed Sri Bhagavan would wait till she came so as not to disappoint her.

With all the grief she had passed through and the peace she had found, she was still mother enough to form a new attachment, and she adopted a daughter, not without asking Sri Bhagavan's permission. When the time came she arranged her marriage and rejoiced at the birth of a grandson whom she named Ramana. And then one day, utterly unprepared, she received a telegram that her adopted daughter had died. The old grief broke upon her again. She rushed up the hill to Sri Bhagavan with the telegram. He read it with tears in his eyes and, appeased but still sorrowful, she left for the funeral. She returned with the child Ramana and placed him in the arms of Sri Bhagavan. Once more there were tears in his eyes as he held the child and his compassion brought her peace.

Echammal used to practise Yogic concentration into which she had been initiated by a North Indian Guru. She would fix her gaze on the tip of her nose and sit in ecstatic contemplation of the light that appeared before her, sometimes for hours together motionless, oblivious of the body. Sri Bhagavan was told of this but did not reply. Finally she herself told him and he discouraged the practice. "Those lights you see outside yourself are not your real goal. You should aim at realizing the Self and nothing short of it." Thereupon she discontinued her former methods and placed her reliance in Sri Bhagavan alone.

Once a Sastri from North India was talking with Sri Bhagavan at Virupaksha Cave when Echammal arrived with food, looking agitated and shivering. When asked what was the matter she said that as she was passing Sadguruswami Cave she thought she saw Sri Bhagavan and a stranger standing beside the path. She continued on her way but heard a voice, "Why go farther up when I am here?" She turned again to look and there was no one there. She hastened on to the Ashram in fear.

"What, Swami!" Sastri exclaimed. "While you are talking to me here you manifest yourself to this lady on the way here and do not show any such sign of Grace to me." And Sri Bhagavan explained that Echammal's visions were due to her constant concentration on him.

She was by no means alone in having visions of Sri Bhagavan though I know of no other case when the vision caused fear. Years later a Western visitor, an elderly gentleman, had come to the Ashram at the foot of the hill. After lunch he set out to explore the hill, but in doing so he lost his way. Tired with the heat and exertion, not knowing which way to go, he was in a desperate plight, when Sri Bhagavan came past and showed him the way back to the Ashram. People were already anxious when he got back and asked him what had happened. "I just went out for a stroll on the hill," he told them, "and got lost. The heat and exertion were a little too much for me and I was in a bad way. I don't know what I should have done but for the fact that Bhagavan happened to come that way and directed me to the Ashram." And they were astonished because Bhagavan had never left the hall.

Rudra Raj Pande, Principal of the Tri-Chandra College at Katmandu, Nepal, went with a friend to worship at the great temple in town before leaving Tiruvannamalai.

"The inner temple gates were thrown open and my guide took us into the interior, which was rather dark. A small oiled wick-flame was flickering a few yards in front of us. The young voice of my companion shouted 'Arunachala'. All my attention was directed to the one purpose of seeing the Image or *Lingam* (which symbolises the Supreme Lord, eternal and unmanifest) in the *Sanctum Sanctorum*. But, strange to say, instead of the *Lingam* I see the image of Maharshi Bhagavan Sri Ramana, his smiling countenance, his brilliant eyes looking at me. And what is more strange, it is not one Maharshi that I see, nor two, nor three — in hundreds I see the same smiling countenance, those lustrous eyes, I see them wherever I may look in that *Sanctum Sanctorum*. My eyes catch not the full figure of the Maharshi but only the smiling face, from the chin above. I am in raptures and beside myself with inexpressible joy — that bliss and calmness of mind I then felt how can words describe? Tears of joy flowed down my cheeks. I went to the temple to see Lord Arunachala and I found the living Lord as he graciously revealed himself. I can never forget the deep intimate experience I had in the ancient temple."[1]

Nevertheless, Sri Bhagavan never encouraged interest in visions or desire for them, nor did they occur to all devotees or disciples.

One of the most devoted adherents of Sri Bhagavan at this time was Seshadri Swami, the same Seshadri who had kept schoolboys away when he first came to Tiruvannamalai. He now lived on the hill, lower down than Virupaksha Cave, and paid frequent visits there. He had attained a high spiritual state and had grace and beauty, which shows in the surviving portraits.

---

[1] *Golden Jubilee Souvenir*, 2nd edition, p. 166.

There was something bird-like and aloof about him. He was not often accessible; he would not always speak, and when he did his speech was often enigmatic. He had left home at the age of seventeen and had received initiation into *mantras* (sacred formulae) and *japa* (invocations) that develop occult powers, sometimes sitting up the whole night in a cemetery invoking the Sakti (creative energy).

Not only would he always encourage devotees to go to Ramanaswami, as he called him, but he would on occasion identify himself with him. He could read thoughts and if Sri Bhagavan had told a devotee anything he would say: "I told you so and so why do you ask again?" or "Why don't you do it?" It was only rarely that he would give initiation into some *mantra* and if the supplicant was already a devotee of Ramanaswami he would always refuse, bidding him remain there where was the supreme *upadesa*, the silent guidance.

On one rare occasion he actually exhorted a devotee to undertake active *sadhana*, the quest for enlightenment. It was a certain Subramania Mudali who, together with his wife and mother, used to spend most of his income preparing food for sadhus who had renounced the world. Like Echammal, they took food daily to Sri Bhagavan and his Ashram, and to Seshadri Swami too when they could find him, and yet at the same time Subramania was a landowner and was involved in litigation and trying to increase his property. Seshadri Swami, grieving that one so devoted should be so attached, advised him to give up such cares and devote himself entirely to the service of God and to striving for spiritual development. "You see," he said, "my younger brother has an income of Rs.10,000 and I have an income of Rs.1,000; why shouldn't you try to get an income of at least a hundred?" The 'younger brother' was Ramanaswami

and the 'income' spiritual attainment. When Subramania still
held back, Seshadri Swami became insistent and warned him
that he was committing the mortal sin of slaying a Brahmin.
Having more faith in Sri Bhagavan, Subramania asked him
whether this was true, and Sri Bhagavan interpreted, "Yes, you
can be said to commit the murder of Brahman by not realizing
that you are Brahman."

Seshadri Swami once sat in the Mango Tree Cave gazing
fixedly at Sri Bhagavan in order to read his thoughts; however
the mind of Sri Bhagavan, merged in the tranquillity of the
Spirit, showed no ripple of thought, so he was baffled and said,
"It is not clear what this person is thinking."

Sri Bhagavan remained silent. After a pause Seshadri
Swami added, "If one worships the Lord Arunachala he will
grant salvation."

And then Bhagavan asked, "Who is it that worships and
who is the worshipped?"

Seshadri Swami broke into a laugh, "That is just what is
not clear."

Then Sri Bhagavan expounded at length the doctrine of
the One Self manifested in all the forms of the universe and yet
unmanifested and utterly unchanged by manifestation, the one
Reality and the Self of him who worships. Seshadri Swami
listened patiently and at the end he rose and said: "I can't say.
All this is dark to me. At any rate I worship."

So saying he turned to the crest of the hill and prostrated
himself to it again and again and then departed.

And yet Seshadri Swami also would sometimes speak from
the standpoint of Unity, seeing all things as manifestations of
the Spirit: but from whatever point of view he spoke it was liable
to be with a dry, disconcerting humour. One day a certain

Narayanaswami found him standing staring at a buffalo and asked, "What is Swami looking at?"

"I am looking at this."

"Is it the buffalo Swami is looking at?" he persisted.

And then, pointing at the buffalo, Seshadri Swami bade him, "Tell me what this is."

"It is a buffalo," he answered innocently, whereupon Seshadri Swami burst out: "Is it a buffalo? A buffalo? You buffalo! Call it Brahman!" So saying he turned and went away.

Seshadri Swami died in January 1929. As is the accepted practice in the case of a Saint, his body was not cremated but buried. Sri Bhagavan stood by silently watching. He is still revered at Tiruvannamalai and on the anniversary of his death his portrait is taken in procession through the town.

During the early years that Sri Bhagavan spent on the hill the process of return to outer activity was gradually proceeding. He began to walk about and explore the hill, to read books and write interpretations. A certain Padmanabha Swami, known also as Jatai Swami on account of his matted hair, had an ashram on the hill and kept there a number of Sanskrit books on spiritual knowledge and on applied sciences with a spiritual basis, such as *ayurveda* (traditional Hindu medicine). Sri Bhagavan would visit him and glance through them, immediately mastering their content and so fixing it in his memory that he could not merely repeat it but give chapter and verse. Padmanabha Swami would often appeal to him as an authority when any point of doctrine was raised.

It is said in the *Puranas* that on the northern slope of Arunachala, near the summit, a *Siddha Purusha* (Sage with supernatural powers) known as Arunagiri Yogi sits beneath a banyan tree, in an almost inaccessible spot, teaching in silence.

There is a shrine or *mantapam* dedicated to him in the Great Temple of Tiruvannamalai. The story indicates that the Grace of Arunachala, guiding men through *mouna diksha* (silent initiation) on the path of Self-enquiry to Liberation, though ever potent, had become inaccessible to the people of this spiritually dark age. Nevertheless, the symbolical meaning of the story does not make it any the less true literally. It happened one day, about 1906, that Sri Bhagavan was wandering on the northern slope of the hill when, in a dry watercourse, he saw an enormous banyan leaf, large enough to serve a meal on. Presuming that it must have been carried down by the water and wishing to see the tree which bore such leaves, he set out on a later occasion to climb the water-course up the hillside. After climbing steep and rugged parts of the hill, he reached a place whence he could see a large flat rock and on it the banyan tree he was seeking, enormous and a deep green. He was amazed to see such a tree growing on what looked like bare rock. He continued to climb but, as he was drawing nearer, disturbed a hornets' nest with his leg. The hornets flew out and attacked the offending leg in a fury of revenge. Sri Bhagavan stood still until they had finished, meekly accepting their just punishment for having destroyed their home; but he took this as a sign not to proceed and so returned to the cave. The devotees were getting anxious as he had been out so long. When they saw him they were appalled at the state of his leg, swollen and inflamed. He has since pointed out the position of the almost inaccessible banyan tree but he never again set out to reach it and he discouraged any of his devotees who wished to do so.

A group of devotees, among them an Englishman, Thomson by name, did once set out determined to find it. After climbing rather recklessly for some time they found themselves in so precarious a position that they dared proceed neither up nor down. They prayed to Bhagavan for help and somehow got back to the Ashram safely. They never tried it again. Others also have made the attempt but without success.

Even though Sri Bhagavan might disapprove of an action it was very seldom that he would explicitly forbid it. Understanding as to what was appropriate or inappropriate had to come from within. In the present case, it was clearly not appropriate for his devotees to attempt what their Master had refrained from.

There was a time when Sri Bhagavan used to roam the hill frequently as well as climbing to the summit and making *pradakshina* (circuit), so that he knew every part of it. And then one day, when he was wandering alone, he passed an old woman gathering fuel on the hillside. She looked like a common outcaste woman, but she addressed the young Swami fearlessly, as an equal. Beginning with the rough cursing common to such people, she said: "May you be put on the funeral pyre! Why do you wander about in the sun like that? Why don't you sit quiet?"

"It can have been no ordinary woman," Sri Bhagavan said when he told the devotees about it; "who knows who she was?" Certainly, no ordinary outcaste woman would have dared to speak to a Swami like that. The devotees took it to be a manifestation of Arunagiri Siddha, the Spirit of Arunachala. From that time Sri Bhagavan gave up roaming the hillside.

When Sri Bhagavan first went to Tiruvannamalai he sometimes moved about in a state of trance, as already described. This did not completely end until about 1912 when there was a final and complete experience of death. He set out from Virupaksha Cave one morning for Pachaiamman Koil, accompanied by Palaniswami, Vasudeva Sastri and others. He had an oil-bath there and was nearing Tortoise Rock on the way back when a sudden physical weakness overcame him. He described it fully afterwards.

"The landscape in front of me disappeared as a bright white curtain was drawn across my vision and shut it out. I could distinctly see the gradual process. There was a stage when I could still see a part of the landscape clearly while the rest was covered by the advancing curtain. It was just like drawing a slide across one's view in a stereoscope. On experiencing this I stopped walking lest I should fall. When it cleared I walked on. When darkness and faintness came over me a second time I leaned against a rock until it cleared. The third time it happened I felt it safer to sit, so I sat down near the rock. Then the bright white curtain completely shut off my vision, my head was swimming and my circulation and breathing stopped. The skin turned a livid blue. It was the regular death hue and it got darker and darker. Vasudeva Sastri, in fact, took me to be dead and held me in his arms and began to weep aloud and lament my death.

"I could distinctly feel his clasp and his shivering and hear his words of lamentation and understand their meaning. I also saw the discolouration of my skin and felt the stoppage of my circulation and breathing and the increased chilliness of the extremities of my body. My usual current of awareness still continued in that state also. I was not in the least afraid and felt no sadness at the condition of the body. I had sat down near the rock in my usual posture and closed my eyes and was not leaning against the rock. The body, left without circulation or respiration, still maintained that position. This state continued for some ten or fifteen minutes. Then a shock passed suddenly through the body and circulation revived with enormous force, and breathing also, and the body perspired from every pore. The colour of life reappeared on the skin. I then opened my eyes and got up and said, 'Let's go'. We reached Virupaksha Cave without further trouble. This was the only fit I had in which both circulation and respiration stopped."

Later, to correct wrong accounts that began to be spread, he added:

"I did not bring on the fit purposely, nor did I wish to see what this body would look like after death, nor did I say that I will not leave this body without warning others. It was one of those fits that I used to get occasionally, only this time it took a very serious form."

What is, perhaps, most striking about this experience is that it was a repetition, heightened by actual physical demonstration, of that certainty of endurance through death which had constituted Sri Bhagavan's spiritual awakening. It recalls the verse from Thayumanavar, the Tamil classic which Sri Bhagavan often quoted: "When overpowered by the wide Expanse which is without beginning, end or middle, there is the realization of non-dual bliss."

It may be that this marked the final completion of Sri Bhagavan's return to full outer normality. It is hard to give any impression of how normal and how human he was in his mode of life, and yet it is necessary, for the description of his previous austerity may leave the idea of someone grim and forbidding. On the contrary, his manner was natural and free from all constraint and the newcomer immediately felt at his ease with him. His conversation was full of humour and his laughter so infectious, so like that of a child, that even those who did not understand the language would join in. Everything about him and about the Ashram was clean and tidy. When a regular Ashram had been established, life in it followed a timetable as exact as work in an office. The clocks were kept right to the minute, the calendars were up-to-date. And nothing was wasted. I have seen an attendant reproved for bringing out a new sheet of paper to bind a book when one already cut into could be made to do. And with food too: not a grain of rice remained on his leaf-plate when he finished eating. Vegetable peelings were saved for the cattle, not thrown away.

There was a spontaneous simplicity and humility about him. One of the few things that aroused a show of anger in him was if those who were serving food gave more of any delicacy to him than to others. He did not like people to rise when he entered the hall but would make a little gesture to them to remain seated. He was walking slowly down the hillside to the Ashram one afternoon, tall, golden-hued, white-haired already and frail, stooping a little and leaning heavily on a staff on account of rheumatism, with him a short, dark attendant. A devotee was coming behind so he drew to the side of the path, saying, "You are younger and walk quicker; you go first." A little courteous action, but so much from Master to disciple.

One could go on endlessly. Some of these points will come up more fittingly later, but now that there is mention of full return to a normal mode of life it has to be indicated how normal, how intensely human and how gracious that mode of life was.

7
NON-
RESISTANCE

NON-RESISTANCE may seem impracticable in an established religion, since every country must have its law courts and police and, at least in modern conditions, its army. However, a religion has two levels of obligation: the minimum obligation upon all who follow it and upon countries where it is established, and the full obligation upon those who devote their lives to following the path laid down, regarding all worldly advantages as nothing in the search for blessedness. It is only in this second and higher sense that Sri Bhagavan established a path, and therefore, for himself and his followers, he could say, "resist not evil". It was no social law for a whole community that he was proclaiming but a way of life for those who followed him. It is possible only for those who have submitted to God's

Will and accept whatever comes as right and necessary even though it may be a misfortune from worldly standards. Sri Bhagavan once said to a devotee, "You thank God for the good things that come to you but you don't thank Him for the things that seem to you bad; that is where you go wrong."

It may be objected that this simple faith is very different from the doctrine of Oneness that Sri Bhagavan taught, but it is only on the mental plane that such theories may conflict. He said, "Submission to God, Guru or Self is all that is needed." As will be shown in a later chapter, these three modes of submission are really not different. It is enough to say here that for one who can hold to the view that there is only the One Self all outer activity appears a dream or cinema-show enacted on the substratum of the Self, so that he will remain an impassive witness. This was the attitude of Sri Bhagavan on the few occasions when evil or molestation threatened.

There were tamarind trees outside Gurumurtam and when he was living there he would sometimes sit under one of them. One day, when no one else was about, a party of thieves came to carry away the ripe tamarind pods. Seeing the young Swami sitting silent at the foot of a tree, one of them said, "Get some acid sap and put it in his eyes; let's see if that will make him speak." It is a sap that might blind a man, apart from the fierce pain it would cause, but he sat motionless, equally unconcerned about his eyes and about the tamarind fruit. Another of the party answered: "Oh, don't bother about him! What harm can he do? Let's get along."

There was occasional interference or opposition during the early years on the Hill. In the strange world of sadhus, where some are frauds and some have striven on the way and developed psychic powers without burning out their lower passions, it was to be expected that the radiance of Divinity recognised by devotees in one so young in years should awaken resentment in a few, though most bowed down and sought his Grace.

Living in a cave on the hill was an elderly sadhu who had shown great reverence for Sri Bhagavan as long as he was at Gurumurtam. After coming to Virupaksha, Sri Bhagavan would sometimes visit him and sit in silence with him. He led a life of austerity and had followers; nevertheless so far was he from having overcome human passions that he could not endure to see the number of the young Swami's followers increase and his own diminish. Deciding to kill Sri Bhagavan or frighten him away from the hill, he took to hiding on the hillside above Virupaksha after sundown and dislodging rocks and stones so that they would roll down there. Sri Bhagavan sat unperturbed although one stone came quite close to him. Always observant, he knew well what was happening and on one occasion he quickly and silently climbed the hill and caught the old man in the act. Even then the latter tried to laugh it off as a joke.

Having failed in this attempt, the sadhu enlisted the aid of Balananda, a plausible scoundrel, handsome and well read, who imposed on people under the guise of a sadhu. This person decided to make profit and prestige out of Sri Bhagavan. Rightly deeming that the young Swami would be too saintly to resist evil, he started posing as his Guru. He would say to visitors: "This young Swami is my disciple," or "Yes, give the child some sweets"; and to Sri Bhagavan, "Here, Venkataraman, my child, take the sweets." Or he would keep up the farce by going into town to buy things for his so-called disciple. Such was his effrontery that he would say blatantly to Sri Bhagavan when alone with him: "I will say I am your Guru and get money from the visitors. It is no loss to you so don't contradict me."

This man's arrogance and offensiveness knew no bounds and one night he went to the length of relieving himself on the veranda of the cave. Next morning he went out early leaving his spare clothes — some of them silk with lace borders — in the cave. Sri Bhagavan said nothing. He went on a long walk to one of the sacred tanks that morning with Palaniswami and before they started Palaniswami washed the veranda, threw out Balananda's clothes and locked up the cave.

Balananda was furious when he returned. He stormed at Palaniswami for daring to touch his clothes and ordered Sri Bhagavan to send him away immediately. Neither of them answered or paid any attention. In his fury Balananda spat on Sri Bhagavan. Even then Sri Bhagavan sat impassive. The disciples who were with him also sat quiet without reacting. However, a devotee from a cave lower down heard of it and rushed up shouting: "You! You dare spit on our Swami!" and could barely be restrained from setting upon the rascal. Balananda decided that he had gone farther than was safe and had better leave Tiruvannamalai. He pronounced the hill not a proper place and departed with his usual arrogance. Going to the railway station he entered a second-class compartment without a ticket. A young couple were in the same compartment. He began to lecture the young man and order him about and when the latter took no notice he became offensive and said: "What! you don't listen to me? It is because of your infatuation with this girl that you don't show me due respect." The incensed young man thereupon took off his sandal and used it to give him the thrashing he had so long needed.

After some months Balananda returned and again made himself a nuisance. On one occasion he insisted on sitting looking fixedly into the eyes of Sri Bhagavan in order, as he averred, to give him *nirvikalpa samadhi* (spiritual trance), but what happened was that he himself fell asleep and Sri Bhagavan and his disciples got up and walked away. Soon after this the general attitude towards him became such that he once more deemed it safer to depart.

There was another 'sadhu' also who tried to gain prestige by posing as the young Swami's Guru. Returning from Kalahasti, he said: "I have come all this way just to see how you are getting on. I will initiate you into the Dattatreya *mantra*."

Sri Bhagavan neither moved nor spoke, so he continued, "God appeared to me in a dream and ordered me to give you this *upadesa*."

"Well then," Sri Bhagavan retorted, "let God appear to me also in a dream and order me to take the *upadesa* and I will take it."

"No, it is very short — just a few letters; you can begin now."

"What use will your *upadesa* be to me unless I go on with the *japa* (invocation)? Find a suitable disciple for it. I am not one."

Some time later, when this sadhu was in meditation, a vision of Sri Bhagavan appeared before him and said, "Don't be deceived!" Frightened and thinking that Sri Bhagavan must possess powers which he was using against him, the sadhu hastened to Virupaksha to apologise and begged to be set free from the apparition. Sri Bhagavan assured him that he used no powers and the sadhu saw there was no anger or resentment.

Another such attempt at interference was by a group of drunken sadhus. Appearing one day at Virupaksha Cave, they solemnly declared: "We are sadhus from Podikai Hill, the sacred hill on which the ancient Agastya Rishi is still doing *tapas* (practising austerities) as he has for thousands of years. He has ordered us to take you first to the Siddhas' Conference at Srirangam and from there to Podikai to give you regular *diksha* (initiation) after extracting from your body those salts that prevent your attaining higher powers."

Sri Bhagavan, as on all such occasions, made no response. However, on this occasion, one of his devotees, Perumalswami, outbluffed the bluffers. He said, "We have already received intimation of your coming and have been commissioned to put your bodies in crucibles and heat the crucibles over a fire." And turning to another devotee he bade him, "Go and dig a pit where we can make a fire for these people." The visitors left in a hurry.

In 1924, when Sri Bhagavan was already living in the present Ashram at the foot of the hill, some thieves broke into the shed that at that time housed his mother's *samadhi* and carried away a few things. A few weeks later three thieves robbed the Ashram itself.

It was on June 26th, at about half past eleven. The night was dark. Sri Bhagavan had already retired to rest on the raised platform in the hall in front of the Mother's *samadhi*. Four devotees were sleeping on the floor near the windows. Two of them, Kunjuswami and Mastan, the former an attendant, heard someone outside say, "There are six persons lying down inside."

Kunju shouted out, "Who's there?"

The thieves replied by breaking a window, apparently to frighten those inside. Kunjuswami and Mastan got up and went to the dais where Sri Bhagavan was. The thieves thereupon broke a window at that side, but Sri Bhagavan sat unperturbed. Kunjuswami then left the hall by the north door, as the thieves were on the south side, and brought Ramakrishnaswami, a

devotee who was sleeping in another hut, to help them. When
he opened the door the two Ashram dogs, Jackie and Karuppan,
ran out. The thieves beat them and Jackie and ran away while
Karuppan ran back to the hall for refuge.

Sri Bhagavan told the thieves that there was very little for
them to take but they were welcome to come in and take what
there was. Either considering this a trap or being too stupid to
depart from routine, they took no notice but continued their
efforts to dislodge a window-frame so as to get in that way.
(According to the usual Indian practice, the windows had iron
bars to prevent anyone getting in). Angered by their wanton
destruction, Ramakrishnaswami sought Bhagavan's permission
to challenge them, but Bhagavan forbade him, saying: "They
have their *dharma* (role), we have ours. It is for us to bear and
forbear. Let us not interfere with them."

Though Sri Bhagavan invited them to enter by the door,
the thieves continued their violent methods. They let off crackers
at the window to give the impression that they had firearms.
Again they were told to enter and take what they wanted but
they only replied with threats. Meanwhile Kunjuswami had left
the hall and set out for town to get help.

Ramakrishnaswami again spoke to the thieves and told
them not to make unnecessary trouble but simply to take what
they wanted. In reply they threatened to set fire to the thatched
room. Sri Bhagavan told them they should not do that but
offered to go out and leave the hall to them. This was just
what they wanted, perhaps still fearing that the others might
set upon them while they were at their work. Sri Bhagavan
first told Ramakrishnaswami to carry the dog, Karuppan, to a
safe place in the other shed for fear the thieves would beat it if
it were left there. Then he with the three others, Mastan,

Thangavelu Pillai and Munisami, a boy who performed puja or worship at the Ashram, left by the north door. The thieves stood at the doorway with sticks and beat them as they went out, either hoping to disable them or to frighten them from any thought of resistance. Sri Bhagavan, receiving a blow on the left thigh, said, "If you are not satisfied you can strike the other leg also." Ramakrishnaswami, however, got back in time to ward off further blows.

Sri Bhagavan and the devotees sat in the thatched shed (later demolished) that stood to the north of the hall. The thieves shouted to them to stay there. "If you move away we'll break your heads!"

Sri Bhagavan told them, "You have the entire hall to yourselves; do what you like."

One of the thieves came and demanded a hurricane lamp and Ramakrishnaswami, on Sri Bhagavan's instructions, gave him a lighted lamp. Again one of them came and asked for the cupboard keys but Kunjuswami had taken them away with him and he was told so. They broke open the cupboards and found there a few thin strips of silver for adorning the images, a few mangoes and a little rice altogether worth about Rs.10. A sum of Rs.6 belonging to Thangavelu Pillai was also taken.

Disappointed with their small takings, one of the thieves returned, brandishing his stick and asking: 'Where is your money? Where do you keep that?"

Sri Bhagavan told him, "We are poor sadhus living on charity and never have cash," and the thief, despite his continued blustering, had to be satisfied with that.

Sri Bhagavan advised Ramakrishnaswami and the others to go and put ointment on their bruises.

"And what about Swami?" Ramakrishnaswami asked.

Sri Bhagavan laughed and replied, "I also have received some puja," punning on the word that could mean either 'worship' or 'blows'.

Seeing the weal on his thigh, Ramakrishnaswami felt a sudden wave of anger. He picked up an iron bar that was lying there and asked for permission to go and see what the thieves were doing, but Sri Bhagavan dissuaded him. "We are sadhus. We should not give up our *dharma*. If you go and strike them some may die and that will be a matter for which the world will rightly blame not them but us. They are only misguided men and are blinded by ignorance, but let us note what is right and stick to it. If your teeth suddenly bite your tongue do you knock them out in consequence?"

It was two o'clock in the morning when the thieves left. A little later Kunjuswami returned with a village officer and two police constables. Sri Bhagavan was still sitting in the northern shed, speaking to his devotees of spiritual matters. The constables asked him what had happened and he simply remarked that some foolish persons had broken into the Ashram and gone away disappointed at finding nothing worth their trouble. The constables made an entry to this effect and went away together with the village officer. Munisami ran after them and told them that the Swami and others had been beaten by the thieves. In the morning the Circle Inspector, Sub-Inspector and a Head Constable came to investigate and later the Deputy Superintendent came. Sri Bhagavan spoke to none about his injury or about the theft except when asked. A few days later some of the stolen property was recovered and the thieves were arrested and sentenced to terms of imprisonment.

8
THE MOTHER

SHORTLY AFTER Sri Bhagavan's mother returned from her unsuccessful attempt to win him back to her in 1900, she lost her eldest son. Two years later the youngest son, Nagasundaram, still only a lad of seventeen, went to Tiruvannamalai for the first time to see his Swami brother. So overcome was he that he embraced him and wept aloud; Sri Bhagavan sat silent, unmoved. The mother came once for a brief visit on her return from a pilgrimage to Benares. In 1914 she went on a pilgrimage to Venkataramanaswami Shrine at Tirupati and again stayed at Tiruvannamalai on her way back. This time she fell ill there and suffered severely for several weeks with symptoms of typhoid. Sri Bhagavan tended her with great solicitude. The verses he composed during her sickness are the only instance known of any prayer of his to influence the course of events.

> Oh Lord! Hill of my refuge, who curest the ills of recurrent births, it is for Thee to cure my mother's fever.
>
> Oh God who slayest death! Reveal Thy feet in the Heart-Lotus of her who bore me to take refuge at Thy Lotus-Feet, and shield her from death. What is death if scrutinised?
>
> Arunachala, Thou blazing fire of Knowledge! Enfold my mother in Thy Light and make her one with Thee. What need then for cremation?
>
> Arunachala, Dispeller of illusion! Why dost Thou delay to dispel my mother's delirium? Is there any but Thee to watch as a Mother over one who has sought refuge in Thee and to rescue from the tyranny of karma?

Ostensibly a prayer for the mother to be saved from her fever, this was in reality a prayer to save her also from the vaster fever of illusion and gather her back into Oneness with the Self in Liberation from the delirium of life.

Needless to say, Alagammal recovered. She returned to Manamadura, but after this prayer circumstances conspired to draw her back from the life of the world to that of the Ashram.

The family house at Tiruchuzhi had been sold to meet debts and pay necessary expenses. Her brother-in-law, Nelliappier, had died, leaving the family in none too easy circumstances. In 1915 the wife of her youngest son, Nagasundaram, died, leaving a young son who was adopted by his aunt Alamelu, now married. Alagammal began to feel that the only place left for her in her old age was with her Swami son. Early in 1916 she went to Tiruvannamalai.

At first she stayed for a few days with Echammal. Some of the devotees were against her staying with Sri Bhagavan, fearing that he might leave his abode in silent protest, as he had left home in 1896. However, there was a great difference, for now it was she who had renounced home, not he who was detained there. The majesty of Sri Bhagavan was so awe-inspiring that, despite his gracious manner, when a question like this arose as to what he would wish none presumed to ask him directly. Even if any did he might sit unmoved, not replying, for he had no wishes. The wish for the mother's recovery expressed in his verses is something quite exceptional.

Soon after his mother came to stay with him, Sri Bhagavan moved from Virupaksha to Skandashram, a little higher up the hill and directly above Virupaksha. This is a much more spacious cave and was constructed for him to occupy. Finding a damp patch of rock there he rightly guessed that there must be a concealed spring. This was released by digging and yielded a perennial flow of water, enough for all Ashram needs, even for a small garden that was made in front of the Cave. The mother began to prepare meals, and so began a new epoch in Ashram life.

Wishing to draw her younger son also to the Ashram, Alagammal sent a devotee to summon him there. He gave up the job he had at Tiruvengadu and went to live at Tiruvannamalai. At first he stayed in town, taking food at the house of some friend or other and daily visiting the Ashram. Before long he took the vow of renunciation and donned the ochre robe under the name of Niranjanananda Swami, although he was more often known familiarly as 'Chinnaswami', the 'Little Swami', through being the brother of the Swami. For a while he still went daily to beg his food in town, but then it seemed incongruous to the devotees that the Swami's own brother should go and beg when there was food for all at the Ashram and he was prevailed upon so settle there.

It was almost as though Sri Bhagavan had reverted to family life, the family having extended to embrace all his devotees; and indeed, he did sometimes refer to them as the family. It was the apparent incongruity of this that at first deterred both his mother and his brother from coming to live with him. Seshadri Swami once referred to it in his droll manner. A visitor who had stopped to see him wanted to continue up the hill to see Ramanaswami and: "Yes," he said, "go and see. There is a householder up there. You will be given sugar cakes (*laddus*) there."

The point of Seshadri Swami's joke is that it has been usual to consider the state of a householder lower than that of a sadhu, since a sadhu can devote himself entirely to the quest, whereas a householder has worldly preoccupations to attend to. The very act of renouncing home and property is looked upon as a great step forward. Therefore many a devotee asked Sri Bhagavan whether he should make the renunciation. Sri Bhagavan always discouraged it. In the case given below he explained that renunciation is not a withdrawal but a widening of love.

Devotee: I am inclined to give up my job and remain always with Sri Bhagavan.

Bhagavan: Bhagavan is always with you, in you. The Self in you is Bhagavan. It is that you should realize.

D: But I feel the urge to give up all attachments and renounce the world as a *sannyasin.*

B: Renunciation does not mean outward divestment of clothes and so on or abandonment of home. True renunciation is the renunciation of desires, passions and attachments.

D: But single-minded devotion to God may not be possible unless one leaves the world.

B: No; one who truly renounces actually merges in the world and expands his love to embrace the whole world. It would be more correct to describe the attitude of the devotee as universal love than as abandoning home to don the ochre robe.

D: At home the bonds of affection are too strong.

B: He who renounces when he is not yet ripe for it only creates new bonds.

D: Is not renunciation the supreme means of breaking attachments?

B: It may be so for one whose mind is already free from entanglements. But you have not grasped the deeper import of renunciation: great souls who have abandoned the life of the world have done so not out of aversion to family life but because of their large-hearted and all-embracing love for all mankind and all creatures.

D: The family ties will have to go some time so why shouldn't I take the initiative and break them now so that my love can be equal to all?

B: When you really feel that equal love for all, when your heart has so expanded as to embrace the whole of creation, you will certainly not feel like giving up this or that; you will simply drop off from secular life as a ripe fruit does from the branch of a tree. You will feel that the whole world is your home.

It is no wonder that such questions came frequently and that many were surprised at the answers they got, because Sri Bhagavan's attitude was contrary to the traditionally accepted point of view. Although the spiritual truths handed down through the ages never vary, the Masters do adapt the modes of training leading to realization of Truth to suit the changed conditions of the age. In the modern world there are many for whom renunciation or even full observance of orthodoxy is impossible. There are devotees who are businessmen, office workers, doctors, lawyers, engineers, bound in one way or another to the life and manners of a modern city, and yet are seeking Liberation.

The explanation that Sri Bhagavan most frequently gave was that true renunciation is in the mind and is neither achieved by physical renunciation nor impeded by the lack of it.

"Why do you think that you are a householder? Similar thoughts that you are a *sannyasin* will haunt you even if you go out as one. Whether you continue in the household or renounce it and go to the jungle, it is your mind that haunts you. The ego is the source of thought. It creates the body and the world and it makes you think you are a householder. If you renounce you will only substitute the thought of renunciation for that of household and the environment of the jungle for that of the home. But the mental obstacles are always there for you. They even increase greatly in the new surroundings. It is no help to change the environment. The one obstacle is the mind and it must be overcome whether in the home or the jungle. If you can do it in the jungle why not in the home? Therefore why change the environment? Your efforts can be made even now, whatever be the environment."

He also explained that it is not the work done that is an obstacle to *sadhana* but only the attitude of mind in which it is done, and that it is possible to continue one's normal avocation, only without attachment. "The feeling 'I work' is the obstacle," he said in *Maharshi's Gospel;* "ask yourself who works. Remember who you are. Then the work will not bind you. It will go on automatically." In *Day by Day with Bhagavan* by Devaraja Mudaliar a fuller explanation is recorded.

> "It is possible to perform all the activities of life with detachment and regard only the Self as real. It is wrong to suppose that if one is fixed in the Self one's duties in life will not be properly performed. It is like an actor. He dresses and acts and even feels the part he is playing, but he knows really that he is not that character but someone else in real life. In the same way, why should the body-consciousness or the feeling 'I-am-the-body' disturb you once you know for certain that you are not the body but the Self? Nothing that the body does should shake you from abidance in the Self. Such abidance will never interfere with the proper and effective discharge of whatever duties the body has, any more than the actor's being aware of his real status in life interferes with his acting a part on the stage."

Just as meditation or remembrance, whichever one calls it, does not impair the work done, so also work done does not impair meditation. Sri Bhagavan explained this clearly in a conversation with Paul Brunton.

B: The life of action need not be renounced. If you meditate for an hour or two every day you can then carry on with your duties. If you meditate in the right manner, then the current of mind induced will continue to flow even in the midst of your work. It is as though there were two ways of expressing the same idea; the same line which you take in meditation will be expressed in your activities.

PB: What will be the result of doing that?

B: As you go on you will find that your attitude towards people, events and objects will gradually change. Your actions will tend to follow your meditation of their own accord.

A man should surrender the personal selfishness which binds him to this world. Giving up the false self is the true renunciation.

PB: How is it possible to become selfless while leading a life of worldly activity?

B: There is no conflict between work and wisdom.

PB: Do you mean that one can continue all the old activities, in one's profession, for instance, and at the same time get Enlightenment?

B: Why not? But in that case one will not think that it is the old personality which is doing the work because one's consciousness will gradually become transformed until it enters in That which is beyond the little self.

Many were puzzled at first by the injunction to work with detachment and wondered whether their work really could be carried on efficiently in such a way. And yet they had before them the example of Sri Bhagavan himself, for whatever he did was meticulously accurate, whether correcting proofs or binding a book, whether preparing food or cutting and polishing a coconut-shell spoon. And in fact, even before the I-am-the-doer illusion has been dissipated, an aloof attitude to work does not impair but enhance efficiency, so long as it is combined with conscientiousness, for it does not imply indifference to the quality of the work done but only non-intrusion of ego into it; and it is the intrusion of ego that causes both friction and inefficiency. If all people were to perform their work simply because it is their work, without vanity or self-interest, exploitation would cease, effort would be rightly directed, co-ordination would replace rivalry, and most of the world's problems would be solved. That the efficiency of the work done would not suffer is apparent if one remembers that the ages of faith in every religion have produced the most exquisite art, whether in Gothic, cathedral or in mosque, whether Hindu sculpture or Taoist painting, by artists who regarded themselves as instruments and preferred to remain anonymous. Examples can be drawn from other professions also. A doctor works more efficiently when he is unemotional and indeed, for this reason, often prefers not to treat his own family. A financier works more coolly and efficiently where his own interests are not at stake. Even in games, fortune favours one who is unconcerned.

The injunction to continue home life sometimes led to the objection that Sri Bhagavan himself had left his home. To this he would answer curtly that every man acts according to his *prarabdha* (destiny). However, it does call for consideration that the full outer normality and participation in the daily routine of life which Sri Bhagavan exemplified so perfectly in later years and which he enjoined upon his followers was not possible for himself immediately after the Awakening at his uncle's house at Madura. The answer is that what had become possible for Sri Bhagavan he, by his Grace, makes possible for those who follow him.

To return to the mother: it was a severe training that she received. Often enough Sri Bhagavan would ignore her, not answering when she spoke, although he took notice of others. If she complained he would say, "All women are my mothers, not you only." One is reminded of Christ's saying when he was told that his mother and brothers were standing at the edge of the crowd, waiting to speak to him, "Whoever does the will of my Father Who is in heaven is my brother and sister and mother." At first Sri Bhagavan's mother would often weep with vexation but gradually understanding developed in her. The feeling of superiority in being the mother of the Swami fell away, the sense of ego was weakened and she devoted herself to the service of the devotees.

Even now, he would still make fun of her orthodox scruples. If her sari happened to touch a non-Brahmin he would exclaim in mock consternation: "Look! Purity is gone! Religion is gone!" The Ashram food was strictly vegetarian, but Alagammal, like some very devout Brahmins, went still further and considered some vegetables also *unsattvic*[1] (impure), and Sri Bhagavan would say mockingly: "Mind that onion! It is a great obstacle to Moksha (Deliverance)!"

It should be said here that Sri Bhagavan did not disapprove of orthodoxy in general. In this case there was excessive attachment to the forms of orthodoxy and that was what he attacked. In general he laid stress on the importance of *sattvic* (pure) food. He did not often give any injunctions at all concerning outer activity; his usual method was to sow the spiritual seed in the heart and leave it to shape the outer life as it grew. The injunctions came from within. One Western devotee was an out-and-out meat-eater when he arrived, looking upon meat as the real substance of a meal as well as the most tasty part, and, with no word spoken on the subject, the time came when he felt an aversion to the very idea of eating meat.

It should be explained in parenthesis, for non-Hindu readers, that the practice of vegetarianism is not only out of disinclination to take life or eat flesh, though that is one reason for it; it is also because *unsattvic* food (which includes some

---

[1] See glossary under *sattvic*.

kinds of vegetables as well as meat) tends to increase animal passions and impede spiritual effort.

There were other ways also in which the mother was made to realize that he who had been born her son was a Divine Incarnation. Once as she sat before him he disappeared and she saw instead a lingam (column) of pure light. Thinking this to mean that he had discarded his human form, she burst into tears, but soon the lingam vanished and he reappeared as before. On another occasion she saw him garlanded and surrounded with serpents like the conventional representations of Siva. She cried to him: "Send them away! I am frightened of them!"

After this she begged him to appear to her henceforth only in his human form. The purpose of the visions had been served; she had realized that the form she knew and loved as her son was as illusory as any other he might assume.

In 1920 the health of the mother began to fail. She was able to work less in the service of the Ashram and was obliged to rest more. During her illness Sri Bhagavan attended on her constantly, often sitting up at night with her. In silence and meditation her understanding matured.

The end came in 1922 on the festival of Bahula Navami, which fell that year on May 19th. Sri Bhagavan and a few others waited on her the whole day without eating. About sunset a meal was prepared and Sri Bhagavan asked the others to go and eat, but he himself did not. In the evening a group of devotees sat chanting the Vedas beside her while others invoked the name of Ram. For more than two hours she lay there, her chest heaving and her breath coming in loud gasps, and all this while Sri Bhagavan sat beside her, his right hand on her heart and his left on her head. This time there was no question of prolonging life but only of quieting the mind so that death could be *Mahasamadhi*, absorption in the Self.

At eight o'clock in the evening she was finally released from the body. Sri Bhagavan immediately rose, quite cheerful. "Now we can eat," he said; "come along, there is no pollution."

There was deep meaning in this. A Hindu death entails ritualistic pollution calling for purificatory rites, but this had not been a death but a reabsorption. There was no disembodied soul but perfect Union with the Self and therefore no purificatory rites were needed. Some days later Sri Bhagavan confirmed this: when someone referred to the passing away of the mother he corrected him curtly, "She did not pass away, she was absorbed."

Describing the process afterwards, he said: "Innate tendencies and the subtle memory of past experiences leading to future possibilities became very active. Scene after scene rolled before her in the subtle consciousness, the outer senses having already gone. The soul was passing through a series of experiences, thus avoiding the need for rebirth and making possible Union with the Spirit. The soul was at last disrobed of the subtle sheaths before it reached the final Destination, the Supreme Peace of Liberation from which there is no return to ignorance."

Potent as was the aid given by Sri Bhagavan, it was the saintliness of Alagammal, her previous renunciation of pride and attachment, that enabled her to benefit by it. He said later: "Yes, in her case it was a success; on a previous occasion I did the same for Palaniswami when the end was approaching, but it was a failure. He opened his eyes and passed away." He added, however, that it was not a complete failure in the case of Palaniswami, for although the ego was not reabsorbed in the Self, the manner of its going was such as to indicate a good rebirth.

Often when devotees suffered bereavement Sri Bhagavan reminded them that it is only the body that dies and only the I-am-the-body illusion that makes death seem a tragedy. Now, at the time of his own bereavement, he showed no grief whatever. The whole night he and the devotees sat up singing devotional songs. This indifference to his mother's physical death is the real commentary on his prayer at the time of her previous sickness.

The question arose of the disposal of the body. There was the testimony of Bhagavan himself that she had been absorbed into the Self and not remained to be reborn to the illusion of ego, but some doubt was felt whether the body of a woman Saint should be given burial instead of being cremated. Then it was recalled that in 1917 this very point had formed part of a series of questions put to Sri Bhagavan by Ganapati Sastri and his party and that he had answered affirmatively. "Since *Jnana* (Knowledge) and *Mukti* (Deliverance) do not differ with the difference of sex, the body of a woman Saint also need not be burnt. Her body also is the abode of God."

In the case of her leaving the Ashram as in that of her joining it, none presumed to ask Sri Bhagavan himself for a decision, nor did he pronounce one. It seems not to have occurred to them that the answer had been given in his prayer of 1914: "Enfold my Mother in Thy Light and make her One with Thee! What need then for cremation?"

Sri Bhagavan stood silently looking on without participating. The body of the mother was interred at the foot of the hill at the southern point, between the Palitirtham Tank and the Dakshinamurti Mantapam (shrine). Relatives and friends arrived for the ceremony and large crowds came from the town. Sacred ashes, camphor, incense, were thrown into the pit around the body before it was filled up. A stone tomb was constructed and on it was installed a sacred lingam brought from Benares. Later a temple was raised on the spot, finally completed in 1949 and known as Matrubhuteswara Temple, the Temple of God Manifested as the Mother.

As the coming of the mother had marked an epoch in Ashram life, so also did her departure. Instead of being checked, the development increased. There were devotees who felt that, as *Shakti* or Creative Energy, her presence was more potent now than before. On one occasion Sri Bhagavan said: "Where has she gone? She is here."

Niranjanananda Swami took up his residence at the foot of the hill near the *samadhi* in a thatched building that was raised there. Sri Bhagavan remained at Skandashram but almost every day he would come down the hillside to the *samadhi,* about half an hour's walk away. Then one day, about six months later, he went out for a walk and, as he was walking, felt a powerful impulse to go down to the *samadhi* and remain there. When he did not return the devotees followed him there and thus was founded Sri Ramanashram. "It was not of my own volition that I moved from Skandashram," he said later, "something brought me here and I obeyed. It was not my decision but the Divine Will."

9
ADVAITA

S RI BHAGAVAN was not a philosopher and there was absolutely no development in his teaching. His earliest expositions, *Self-Enquiry* and *Who Am I?*, are no different in doctrinal theory from those he gave verbally in his last years. When, as a lad of sixteen, he realized his identity with the Absolute, with That which is Pure Being underlying all that is, it was formless, intuitive knowledge of which the doctrinal implications were recognised only later. "I did not yet know that there was an Essence or Impersonal Real underlying everything and that God and I were both identical with it. Later, at Tiruvannamalai, as I listened to the *Ribhu Gita* and other sacred books, I learnt all this and found that they were analysing and naming what I had felt intuitively without analysis or name."

It was no question of opinions but of Truth recognised; that is to say that he was not convinced by what he read but simply recognised its conformity with what he already intuitively knew.

All modes and levels of doctrine are comprised within Hinduism, all of them legitimate and corresponding to the various modes of approach required by people of varying temperament and development. The approach through love and worship of a Personal God exists, as it does in the Western or Semitic religions. So also does the approach through service, seeing God manifested in all His creatures and worshipping Him by serving them. However, the recognition of Pure Being as one's Self and the Self of the universe and of all beings is the supreme and ultimate Truth, transcending all other levels of doctrine without denying their truth on their own plane. This is the doctrine of Advaita, Non-duality, taught by the ancient Rishis and pre-eminently by Shankaracharya. It is the simplest as well as the most profound, being the ultimate truth beyond all the complexities of cosmology.

Non-duality means that only the Absolute is. The entire cosmos exists within the Absolute, having no intrinsic reality but merely manifesting the Absolute which, however, remains eternally unchanged and unmanifest, as the people and events in a man's dream exist within him and have no reality apart from him and yet add nothing to him by their creation and subtract nothing from him by their disappearance. This means that the Absolute is the Self of the cosmos and of every being. Therefore by seeking his Self, by the constant investigation 'Who am I?' it is possible for a man to realize his identity with Universal Being. It was the purest Advaita that Sri Bhagavan taught.

Some may fear that the doctrine of the One Self deprives them of a Personal God to Whom they can pray, but there is no need for such fear, because as long as the reality of the ego who prays endures so long does the reality of the God to Whom he prays; so long as a man accepts his ego as a reality, the world outside it and God above it are also realities for him. This is the level of a dualistic religion and a Personal God. It is true but not the ultimate Truth. "All religions postulate the three fundamentals: individual, God and world. It is only so long as the ego endures that one says either, 'The One manifests Itself as the three' or, 'The three are really three'. The supreme state is to inhere in the Self, the ego extinguished" (*Forty Verses on Reality*, v.2).

Some people also revolt against the conception of the world as unreal, even while admitting the reality of the Spirit, but that is because they have not understood in what sense it is unreal. Sri Bhagavan often explained this, and nowhere more concisely than in the following statement recorded by S.S. Cohen:

> "Shankaracharya has been criticised for his philosophy of Maya (illusion) without understanding his meaning. He made three statements: that Brahman is real, that the universe is unreal, and that Brahman is the universe. He did not stop with the second. The third statement explains the first two; it signifies that when the universe is perceived apart from Brahman that perception is false and illusory. What it amounts to is that phenomena are real when experienced as the Self and illusory when seen apart from the Self."

The teaching of Sri Bhagavan was intensely practical. He expounded theory only in answer to the specific needs and questions of devotees and as a necessary basis for practice. When reminded once (in *Maharshi's Gospel*) that the Buddha had refused to answer questions about God, he replied with approval,

"In fact the Buddha was more concerned with directing the seeker to realize Bliss here and now than with academic discussions about God and so forth." So also, he himself would often refuse to gratify curiosity, turning the questioner instead to the need for *sadhana* or effort. Asked about the posthumous state of man, he might reply: "Why do you want to know what you will be when you die before you know what you are now? First find out what you are now." A man is now and eternally the deathless Self behind this and every other life, but to be told so or to believe it is not enough; it is necessary to strive to realize it. Similarly, if asked about God he might reply: "Why do you want to know about God before you know yourself? First find out what you are."

The process by which this is to be done is described in a later chapter, but since the next chapter already recounts Sri Bhagavan's instructions to devotees, reference is made to it and to his teaching here.

That his teaching was not 'philosophy' in the usual sense of the term may be seen from the fact that (as will appear in his replies to Sivaprakasam Pillai in the next chapter) he did not instruct his devotees to think out problems but to eliminate thought. This may sound as though the process is stupefying, but, as he explained to Paul Brunton in the conversation quoted in Chapter Two, the reverse is true. A man is identical with the Self, which is pure Being, pure Consciousness, pure Bliss, but the mind creates the illusion of a separate individuality. In deep sleep the mind is stilled and a man is one with the Self, but in an unconscious way. In *samadhi* he is one with the Self in a fully conscious way, not in darkness but in light. If the interference of the mind is stilled, the consciousness of Self can, by the Grace of the Guru, awaken in the heart, thus preparing for this blissful

Identity, for a state that is not torpor or ignorance but radiant. Knowledge, pure I-am-ness.

Many may recoil from the idea of destruction of the mind or (what comes to the same thing) of the separate individuality and find it terrifying, and yet it happens to us daily in sleep and, far from being afraid to go to sleep, we find it desirable and pleasant, even though in sleep the mind is stilled only in an ignorant way. In rapture or ecstasy, on the other hand, the mind is momentarily absorbed and stilled in a fragmentary experience of the bliss that is its true nature. The very words indicate the transcending of the individuality, since 'rapture' means etymologically being carried away and 'ecstasy' standing outside oneself. The expression 'it is breath-taking' really means 'it is thought-taking,' for the source of thought and breath is the same, as Sri Bhagavan explained when speaking of breath-control. The truth is that the individuality is not lost but expanded to Infinity.

The elimination of thoughts is for the purpose of concentrating on the deeper awareness that is behind and beyond thought. Far from weakening the mind, it strengthens it, for it teaches concentration. Sri Bhagavan frequently confirmed this. It is the weak and uncontrolled mind that is constantly distracted by irrelevant thoughts and harassed by unhelpful worries; the mind that is strong enough to concentrate, no matter on what, can turn its concentration to the elimination of thoughts in quest of the Self, and conversely, the effort to eliminate thoughts in the manner prescribed gives strength and power of concentration. When the quest is achieved the faculties of the mind are not lost: Sri Bhagavan illustrated this by comparing the mind of the *Jnani* to the moon in the sky at midday — it is illuminated but its light is not needed in the greater radiance of the sun which illuminates it.

10
SOME EARLY DEVOTEES

ALTHOUGH THE DOCTRINE Sri Bhagavan taught never varied, the way of teaching varies according to the character and understanding of the questioner. During the years on the hill, records were kept of the experiences of some of the devotees and of the expositions they received, and a few of these are given below. Indeed, it may be said that the experiences of his devotees constitute the biography of Sri Bhagavan, since he himself was established in the immutability beyond events and experiences.

SIVAPRAKASAM PILLAI

Sivaprakasam Pillai was one of the intellectuals among the devotees. He had taken philosophy at the university and had already pondered over the mysteries of Being. In 1900 he was

appointed to a post in the Revenue Department in South Arcot
District. Two years later his work took him to Tiruvannamalai
and he heard of the young Swami on the Hill. He was captivated
at the very first visit and became a devotee. He put fourteen
questions and, since the Swami was still maintaining silence,
both questions and answers were in writing. The answer to the
first question was written by the Swami on a slate and
immediately copied out by Sivaprakasam Pillai. The other
thirteen were written out later from memory but checked by
Sri Bhagavan before being published.

SP: Swami, who am I? And how is salvation to be attained?
B: By incessant inward enquiry 'Who am I?' you will know
     yourself and thereby attain salvation.
SP: Who am I?
B: The real I or Self is not the body, nor any of the five senses,
     nor the sense-objects, nor the organs of action, nor the
     prana (breath or vital force), nor the mind, nor even the
     deep sleep state where there is no cognisance of these.
SP: If I am none of these what else am I?
B: After rejecting each of these and saying 'this I am not', that
     which alone remains is the 'I', and that is Consciousness.
SP: What is the nature of that Consciousness?
B: It is *Sat-Chit-Ananda* (Being-Consciousness-Bliss) in which
     there is not even the slightest trace of the I-thought. This
     is also called *Mouna* (Silence) or *Atma* (Self). That is the
     only thing that is. If the trinity of world, ego and God are
     considered as separate entities they are mere illusions like
     the appearance of silver in mother of pearl. God, ego and
     world are really Siva *swarupa* (the Form of Siva) or Atma
     swarupa (the form of the Spirit).

SP: How are we to realize that Real?

B: When the things seen disappear the true nature of the seer or subject appears.

SP: Is it not possible to realize That while still seeing external things?

B: No, because the seer and the seen are like the rope and the appearance of a serpent therein. Until you get rid of the appearance of a serpent you cannot see that what exists is only the rope.

SP: When will external objects vanish?

B: If the mind, which is the cause of all thoughts and activities, vanishes, external objects will also vanish.

SP: What is the nature of the mind?

B: The mind is only thoughts. It is a form of energy. It manifests itself as the world. When the mind sinks into the Self then the Self is realized; when the mind issues forth the world appears and the Self is not realized.

SP: How will the mind vanish?

B: Only through the enquiry 'Who am I?' Though this enquiry also is a mental operation, it destroys all mental operations, including itself, just as the stick with which the funeral pyre is stirred is itself reduced to ashes after the pyre and corpses have been burnt. Only then comes Realization of the Self. The I-thought is destroyed, breath and the other signs of vitality subside. The ego and the *prana* (breath or vital force) have a common source. Whatever you do, do without egoism, that is without the feeling 'I am doing this'. When a man reaches that state even his own wife will appear to him as the Universal Mother. True *Bhakti* (devotion) is surrender of the ego to the Self.

SP: Are there no other ways of destroying the mind?

B: There is no other adequate method except Self-enquiry. If the
mind is lulled by other means it stays quiet for a little while
and then springs up again and resumes its former activity.

SP: But when will all the instincts and tendencies (*vasanas*),
such as that to self-preservation, be subdued in us?

B: The more you withdraw into the Self, the more these
tendencies wither, and finally they drop off.

SP: Is it really possible to root out all these tendencies that have
soaked into our minds through many births?

B: Never yield room in your mind for such doubts, but dive
into the Self with firm resolve. If the mind is constantly
directed to the Self by this enquiry it is eventually dissolved
and transformed into the Self. When you feel any doubt
do not try to elucidate it but to know who it is to whom
the doubt occurs.

SP: How long should one go on with this enquiry?

B: As long as there is the least trace of tendencies in your mind
to cause thoughts. So long as the enemy occupy a citadel
they will keep on making sorties. If you kill each one as
he comes out, the citadel will fall to you in the end.
Similarly, each time a thought rears its head crush it with
this enquiry. To crush out all thoughts at their source is
called *vairagya* (dispassion). So *vichara* (Self-enquiry)
continues to be necessary until the Self is realized. What
is required is continuous and uninterrupted remembrance
of the Self.

SP: Is not this world and what takes place therein the result of
God's will? And if so why should God will thus?

B: God has no purpose. He is not bound by any action. The
world's activities cannot affect Him. Take the analogy of
the sun. The sun rises without desire, purpose or effort,

but as soon as it rises numerous activities take place on earth: the lens placed in its rays produces fire in its focus, the lotus bud opens, water evaporates, and every living creature enters upon activity, maintains it, and finally drops it. But the sun is not affected by any such activity, as it merely acts according to its nature, by fixed laws, without any purpose, and is only a witness. So it is with God. Or take the analogy of space or ether. Earth, water, fire and air are all in it and have their modifications in it, yet none of these affects ether or space. It is the same with God. God has no desire or purpose in His acts of creation, maintenance destruction, withdrawal and salvation to which beings are subjected. As the beings reap the fruit of their actions in accordance with His laws, the responsibility is theirs, not God's. God is not bound by any actions.

Sri Bhagavan's saying that the true nature of him who sees appears only when the things seen disappear is not to be taken literally as stipulating unawareness of the physical world. That would be a state of formless trance or *nirvikalpa samadhi*; what is meant is that they cease to appear real and are seen as mere forms assumed by the Self. This is made clear by the example of the rope and the serpent that follows. It is a traditional example, used also by Sri Shankara. A man sees a coiled rope in the dusk and mistakes it for a serpent and is therefore frightened. When day dawns he sees that it was only a rope and that his fear was groundless. The Reality of Being is the rope, the illusion of a serpent that frightened him is the objective world.

The statement that to crush out thoughts at their source is *vairagya* also requires elucidation. The meaning of *vairagya* is dispassion, detachment, equanimity. Sivaprakasam Pillai's question as to when the instincts and latent tendencies in a man

could be subdued shows that it was *vairagya* that he felt the
need to strive after. Sri Bhagavan was, in effect, telling him that
vichara or Self-enquiry is the shortest road to *vairagya*. Passion
and attachment are in the mind; therefore when the mind is
controlled they are subdued, and that is *vairagya*.

These answers were later expanded and arranged in book
form as 'Who Am I?' perhaps the most widely appreciated prose
exposition by Sri Bhagavan.

By 1910 Sivaprakasam Pillai already found government service
irksome and an impediment to *sadhana* or spiritual quest. He was
sufficiently well-to-do to lead the life of a householder without
earning, so he resigned from service. Three years later he was faced
with the real decision, whether his resignation meant withdrawal
from the life of the world or whether he was merely renouncing
what was irksome and retaining what was pleasant. His wife died
and he had to decide whether to marry again or to take up the life
of a sadhu. He was still barely middle aged and there was a girl he
was strongly attracted to. But then the question of money also arose
if he was to marry again and to set up a new household.

He shrank at first from asking Sri Bhagavan about such
matters, perhaps realising in his heart what the reply would be;
so he tried to obtain an answer in another way. He wrote out
four questions on a piece of paper.

1. What am I to do to escape all sorrows and cares on earth?

2. Shall I get married to the girl I am thinking of?

3. If not, why not?

4. If the marriage is to come off, how is the necessary
money to be raised?

With this he proceeded to a temple of Vighneswara, the
aspect of God to which he had been wont to pray from childhood.
He placed the paper before the idol and kept vigil all night,

praying that the answer might appear written on the paper or
that he might receive some sign or vision.

Nothing happened and he had now no other recourse but
to approach the Swami. He went to Virupaksha Cave but still
shrank from putting the questions. Day after day he postponed
doing so. Even though Sri Bhagavan never encouraged anyone
to renounce home life, that did not mean that he would
encourage one whom destiny itself had set free to go back
deliberately for a second dose. Sivaprakasam Pillai gradually felt
the answer borne in upon him from the sight of the Swami's
own life in its serene purity, utterly indifferent to women, utterly
unconcerned about money. The date he had fixed for his
departure arrived with the questions still unasked. There were
many people about that day, so that even if he had still wished
to put his questions he could not without making them public.
He sat gazing on the Swami, and as he gazed he suddenly beheld
a halo of dazzling light about his head and a golden child emerging
from his head and then re-entering. Was it a living reply that
the progeny is not of the flesh but of the Spirit? A flood of
ecstasy came over him. The strain of his long period of doubt
and indecision was broken and he sobbed in pure relief.

It is an illustration of the great normality that prevailed
around Sri Bhagavan that when Sivaprakasam Pillai told the
other devotees what had happened some of them laughed or
were incredulous and some suspected that he had taken a drug.
Although many instances of visions and unusual occurrences
could be culled, they would be spread out very thinly over the
fifty and more years of Sri Bhagavan's manifestation among us.

Overcome with joy, Sivaprakasam Pillai gave up all
thought of leaving that day. The next evening, as he sat before
Sri Bhagavan, he again had a vision. This time Bhagavan's body

shone like the morning sun and round him a halo as of full moons. Then again he saw the entire body covered with sacred ashes and the eyes glowing with compassion. Again two days later he had a vision, this time as though the body of Sri Bhagavan was of pure crystal. He was overwhelmed and feared to leave lest the joy surging in his heart should cease. Eventually he returned to his village, the unasked questions answered. He spent the rest of his life in celibacy and austerity. All these experiences he described in a Tamil poem. He also wrote other poems in praise of Sri Bhagavan, some of which are still sung by the devotees.

NATESA MUDALIAR

Not all comers understood the silent *upadesa* (instruction) of Sri Bhagavan. Natesa Mudaliar did eventually but it took him a long time. He was an elementary school teacher when he read Vivekananda and became fired with eagerness to renounce the world and find a Guru. Friends told him of the Swami on Arunachala Hill but added that it was well-nigh hopeless to seek *upadesa* (guidance) of him. Nevertheless, Mudaliar decided to try. It was in 1918 and Sri Bhagavan was already at Skandashram. Mudaliar went there and sat before him, but Sri Bhagavan remained silent and Mudaliar, not presuming to speak first, came away disappointed.

Having failed in this attempt, he travelled about visiting other Swamis but found none in whom he felt the Divine Presence and to whom he could surrender. After two years' fruitless search he wrote a long letter to Sri Bhagavan imploring him not to be selfishly indifferent to the fate of longing souls and asking permission to come again, since his first visit had been ineffective. A month passed with no reply. Then he sent a registered letter, acknowledgement due, and this time he wrote: "However many rebirths I have to go through, I am determined to receive *upadesa* from you and you alone. So you will have to be reborn for that purpose if you give me up in this life as too unprepared or immature to receive your *upadesa*. I swear to this."

A few days later Sri Bhagavan appeared to him in a dream and said: "Do not think continually of me. You must first obtain the Grace of God Maheswara, the Lord of the Bull. First meditate on him and secure his Grace. My help will follow as a matter of course." He had a picture in his house of God Maheswara riding upon a bull and he took this as a support for meditation. A few days later he received an answer to his letter, "The Maharshi does not reply to letters; you can come and see him in person."

He wrote once more to make sure that the letter was written at Sri Bhagavan's bidding and then set out for Tiruvannamalai. Following the course prescribed in his dream, he went first to the great temple in town, where he had *darshan* (enjoyed the presence) of Lord Arunachaleswar and spent the night. A Brahmin whom he met there tried to dissuade him from his purpose. "Now listen, I have spent sixteen years near Ramana Maharshi trying in vain to obtain his *Anugraham* (Grace). He is indifferent to everything. Even if you break your head there, he will not be interested to ask why. Since it is impossible to obtain his Grace there is no point in your visiting him."

This is a remarkable illustration of the understanding that Sri Bhagavan required of his devotees. Where those whose hearts were open would find him more solicitous than a mother and some would tremble with awe, one who judged by outward signs would find none. Natesa Mudaliar was not the sort of man to be put off. Since he insisted on going, the other told him: "Anyhow, you can find out in this way whether you will have the good luck to obtain his Grace. There is a Swami on the Hill by the name of Seshadri who mixes with none and generally drives away people who try to approach him. It you can obtain some mark of favour from him it will be a good augury for success."

Next morning Mudaliar set out with J.V. Subrahmanya Iyer, a colleague in his profession, in quest of the elusive Seshadri Swami. After much searching they saw him and, to Mudaliar's relief and astonishment, he himself approached them. Without needing to be told their errand, he addressed Mudaliar: "My poor child! Why are you grieved and anxious? What is *Jnana* (Knowledge)? After the mind rejects objects, one after another, as transient and unreal, That which survives this elimination is *Jnana*. That is God. Everything is That and That alone. It is folly to run hither and thither in the belief that *Jnana* can be attained only by going to a hill or a cave. Go without fear." Thus did he give not his *upadesa* (instruction) but that of Sri Bhagavan, in the very words Bhagavan might have used.

Buoyed up by this propitious augury, they proceeded up the hillside to Skandashram. It was about noon when they arrived. For five or six hours Mudaliar sat before Sri Bhagavan and no word passed between them; then the evening meal was ready and Sri Bhagavan rose to go out. J.V.S. Iyer said to him, "This is the man who wrote those letters." Sri Bhagavan thereupon looked fixedly at him and then turned and went out, still without speaking.

Month after month Mudaliar came back for a day and sat there, mutely imploring, but Sri Bhagavan never spoke to him, nor did he presume to speak first. After a full year had elapsed in this way he could endure it no longer and at last he said, "I wish to learn and experience what your Grace is, as people differ in their accounts of it."

Sri Bhagavan replied: "I am always giving my Grace. If you can't apprehend it what am I to do?"

Even now Mudaliar did not understand the silent *upadesa* (guidance); he was still confused as to what path he should follow. Shortly afterwards Sri Bhagavan appeared to him in a dream and said: "Let your vision be unified and withdrawn from objects, both external and internal. Thus, as differences disappear you will progress." Mudaliar understood this to apply to his physical sight and replied: "This does not seem to me the right way. If such a superior person as you gives me advice like this who will give me true advice?" However, Sri Bhagavan assured him that it was the right way.

The next development Mudaliar himself has described: "I followed this dream *upadesa* for a while, then I had another dream. This time Sri Bhagavan appeared to me while my father was standing by and asked, pointing to my father, "Who is this?" With some hesitation about the philosophical accuracy of the answer I replied, "My father". Maharshi smiled at me significantly and I added, "My answer is in accordance with common parlance but not with philosophy", because I remembered that I was not the body. Maharshi drew me to him and placed his palm first on my head and then on my right breast, pressing his finger over the nipple. It was rather painful, but as it was his Grace I endured it quietly. I did not know then why he pressed the right breast instead of the left"[1]

Thus, having failed to receive the silent initiation, he was given, even though in a dream, the initiation by touch.

He was one of those whose eagerness and desire to make every effort drove them to the idea of renouncing home life and

---

[1] The reason for this is given in Chapter Twelve.

going forth as a penniless wanderer. As in other cases, Sri Bhagavan discouraged this. "Just as you avoid the cares of home life when you are here, go home and try to be equally unconcerned and unaffected there." Mudaliar still lacked the full reliance and conviction of a disciple towards his Guru and he made the renunciation despite Sri Bhagavan's clear injunction. He found, as Sri Bhagavan had predicted, that the difficulties on his path grew greater, not less, and after a few years returned to his family and took up work again. After this his devotion deepened. He composed Tamil poems in praise of Sri Bhagavan. And at last he received, more fully than most others, the verbal instructions that he had so longed for, for it was he who was the recipient of a large part of the expositions contained in *A Catechism of Instruction* in which is most beautifully set forth the doctrine of the Guru and his Grace.

GANAPATI SASTRI

Altogether outstanding among the devotees was Ganapati Sastri, known also as Ganapati Muni (*i.e.* 'the Sage Ganapati') and given the honorific title of Kavyakanta (one who has poetry in his throat *i.e,* an extempore poet) for his pre-eminence in Sanskrit extempore verse disputation. He was a man of towering ability that would have placed him in the very forefront of modern writers and scholars had he had the ambition and that would have made him a great Spiritual Master had he totally lacked ambition, but he fell between the two. Too much turned to God to seek success or fame, he was nevertheless too anxious to aid and uplift mankind to escape from the I-am-the-doer illusion.

At the time of his birth in 1878 (one year before that of Sri Bhagavan) his father was at Benares before an image of the God Ganapati and beheld a vision of a child running up to him from the God; therefore he named his child Ganapati. For the first five years of his life Ganapati was dumb and subject to epileptic fits and seemed anything but a promising child. Then he was cured, it seems, by branding with a red-hot iron, and immediately began to display his marvellous ability. By the age of ten he had written Sanskrit verse and prepared an astrological almanac besides mastering several *Kavyas* (Sanskrit works) and grammars. At fourteen he had mastered the *Panchakavyas* and the chief books on Sanskrit prosody and rhetoric, read the *Ramayana* and Mahabharata and some of the *Puranas*. He could already speak and write fluent Sanskrit. Like Sri Bhagavan, he had a phenomenal memory. Whatever he read or heard, he remembered and, again like Sri Bhagavan, he had the ability of *ashtavadhana*, that is of giving his attention to a number of different things at the same time.

The stories of the ancient Rishis fired him with emulation and from the age of eighteen, shortly after his marriage, he began travelling about India, visiting sacred places, repeating mantras (sacred phrases) and performing *tapas* (asceticism). In 1900 he attended a meeting of Sanskrit pandits at Nadiya in Bengal, where his extraordinary facility in impromptu versification and brilliant philosophic disputation won him the title of Kavyakanta already referred to. In 1903 he came to Tiruvannamalai and twice visited the Brahmana Swami on the Hill. For awhile he took a job as school teacher in Vellore, a few hours railway journey from Tiruvannamalai, and there he gathered round him a group of disciples who were to develop their Sakti (power or energy) by the use of mantras to such an extent that the subtle influence would permeate and uplift the whole nation, if not all mankind.

The life of a teacher could not hold him for long. By 1907 he was back again in Tiruvannamalai. But by now doubts began to oppress him. He was approaching middle age and with all his brilliance and vast learning and all his mantras and *tapas* he had not attained success as yet either with God or the world. He felt that he had come to a dead end. On the ninth day of the Kartikai festival he suddenly remembered the Swami on the Hill. Surely he must have the answer. As soon as the impulse came he acted on it. In the heat of the afternoon sun he climbed the hill to Virupaksha Cave. The Swami was sitting alone on the veranda of the cave. Sastri fell on his face before him and clasped his feet with outstretched hands. In a voice quivering with emotion, he said: "All that has to be read I have read; even Vedanta *Sastra* I have fully understood; I have performed *japa* (invocation) to my heart's content; yet have I not up to this time understood what *tapas* is. Therefore I have sought refuge at your feet. Pray enlighten me as to the nature of *tapas*."

The Swami turned his silent gaze upon him for some fifteen minutes and then replied: "If one watches whence the notion 'I' arises, the mind is absorbed into That; that is *tapas*. When a mantra is repeated, if one watches the Source from which the mantra sound is produced the mind is absorbed in That; that is *tapas*."

It was not so much the words spoken that filled him with joy as the Grace radiating from the Swami. With the exuberant vitality that he put into everything, he wrote to friends of the *upadesa* he had received and began composing praises of the Swami in Sanskrit verse. He learned from Palaniswami that the Swami's name had been Venkataramana and declared that henceforth he must be known as Bhagavan Sri Ramana and as the Maharshi. The name 'Ramana' immediately came into use; so also did the title Maharshi (Maha-Rishi, the Great Rishi). It long remained customary to refer to him in speech and writing as 'the Maharshi'. However, the practice gradually prevailed among the devotees of addressing him in the third person as 'Bhagavan', which means 'the Divine' or simply 'God'. He himself usually spoke impersonally, avoiding the use of the word 'I'. For instance, he did not actually say, "I did not know when the sun rose or when it set," as quoted in Chapter Five, but "Who knew when the sun rose or when it set?" Sometimes also he referred to his body as 'this'. Only in making a statement in which the word 'God' would be appropriate did he say 'Bhagavan' and speak in the third person. For instance, when my daughter was going back to school and he was asked to remember her while she was away, the reply was, "If Kitty remembers Bhagavan, Bhagavan will remember Kitty."

Ganapati Sastri also liked to refer to Sri Bhagavan as a manifestation of Lord Subrahmanya; however in this the devotees rightly refused to follow him, feeling that to regard Sri Bhagavan as a manifestation of any one divine aspect was to attempt to limit the illimitable. Nor did Sri Bhagavan countenance the identification. A visitor once said to him, "If Bhagavan is an avatar of Subrahmanya, as some people say, why does he not tell us so openly instead of leaving us to guess?"

And he replied, "What is an avatar? An avatar is only a manifestation of one aspect of God, whereas a *Jnani* is God Himself."

About a year after his meeting with Sri Bhagavan, Ganapati Sastri experienced a remarkable outflow of his Grace. While he was sitting in meditation in the temple of Ganapati at Tiruvothiyur he felt distracted and longed intensely for the presence and guidance of Sri Bhagavan. At that moment Sri Bhagavan entered the temple. Ganapati Sastri prostrated himself before him and, as he was about to rise, he felt Sri Bhagavan's

hand upon his head and a terrifically vital force coursing through
his body from the touch, so that he also received Grace by touch
from the Master.

Speaking about this incident in later years, Sri Bhagavan
said: "One day, some years ago I was lying down and awake
when I distinctly felt my body rise higher and higher. I could
see the physical objects below growing smaller and smaller
until they disappeared and all around me was a limitless
expanse of dazzling light. After some time I felt the body
slowly descend and the physical objects below began to
appear. I was so fully aware of this incident that I finally
concluded that it must be by such means that *Siddhas* (Sages
with powers) travel over vast distances in a short time and
appear and disappear in such a mysterious manner. While
the body thus descended to the ground it occurred to me
that I was at Tiruvothiyur though I had never seen the place
before. I found myself on a highroad and walked along it. At
some distance from the roadside was a temple of Ganapati
and I entered it."

This incident is very characteristic of Sri Bhagavan. It
is characteristic that the distress or devotion of one of his
people should call forth an involuntary response and
intervention in a form that can only be called miraculous,
and it is also characteristic that Sri Bhagavan, with all powers
at his feet, should be no more interested to use powers of
the subtle than of the physical world, and when some such
thing happened in response to the appeal of a devotee should
say with the simplicity of a child, "I suppose that is what
Siddhas do."

It was just this indifference that Ganapati Sastri failed to
attain. He asked once, "Is seeking the source of the I-thought

sufficient for the attainment of all my aims or is mantra *dhyana* (incantation) needed?" Always the same: his aims, his ambitions, the regeneration of the country, the revitalisation of religion.

Sri Bhagavan replied curtly, "The former will suffice." And when Sastri continued about his aims and ideals he added: "It will be better if you throw the entire burden on the Lord. He will carry all the burdens and you will be free from them. He will do his part."

In 1917 Ganapati Sastri and other devotees put a number of questions to Sri Bhagavan and the questions and answers have been recorded in a book entitled *Sri Ramana Gita*, more erudite and doctrinal than most of the books. Characteristically, one of the questions that Ganapati Sastri asked was whether someone who attained *Jnana* (Self-realization), as it were, by the way while seeking some specific powers would find his original desires fulfilled. And nowhere is Sri Bhagavan's swift and subtle humour better illustrated than in the reply he gave, "If the Yogi, though starting upon Yoga for the fulfilment of his desires, gained Knowledge in the meantime he would not be unduly elated even though his desires were likewise fulfilled."

About 1934 Ganapati Sastri settled down in the village of Nimpura near Kharagpur with a group of followers and from then until his death some two years later devoted himself wholly to *tapas* (asceticism). Sri Bhagavan was asked once, after Sastri's death, whether he could have attained Realization during this life, and he replied: "How could he? His *sankalpas* (inherent tendencies) were too strong."

F.H. HUMPHREYS

The first Western devotee of Sri Bhagavan was already grounded in occultism when he came to India in 1911. He was only twenty-one and had come to take up a post in the Police service at Vellore. He engaged a tutor, one Narasimhayya, to teach him Telugu and in the very first lesson asked him whether he could procure a book in English on Hindu astrology. It was a strange request from a white sahib, but Narasimhayya assented and got him one from a library. The next day Humphreys asked an even more astonishing question, "Do you know any Mahatma here?"

Narasimhayya answered briefly that he did not. This did not save him from embarrassment for long, for the next day Humphreys said: "Did you tell me yesterday that you don't know any Mahatma? Well, I saw your Guru this morning just before I woke from sleep. He sat by my side and said something which, however, I did not understand."

As Narasimhayya still seemed unconvinced, Humphreys continued, "The first man from Vellore whom I met at Bombay was you." Narasimhayya began to protest that he had never been to Bombay, but Humphreys explained that as soon as he arrived there he had been taken to hospital in a high fever. In order to gain some relief from pain, he had directed his mind to Vellore, where he should have proceeded immediately on landing but for his illness. He travelled to Vellore in his astral body and saw Narasimhayya there.

Narasimhayya replied simply that he did not know what an astral body was, or any body but a physical one. However, in order to test the truth of the dream he next day left a bundle of photographs on Humphreys' table before going to give a lesson to another police officer. Humphreys looked through them and immediately picked out that of Ganapati Sastri. "There!" he exclaimed when his teacher returned. "That is your Guru."

Narasimhayya admitted that it was. After this Humphreys again fell sick and had to leave for Ootacamund to recuperate.

It was several months before he returned to Vellore. When he did, he again surprised Narasimhayya, this time by sketching a mountain cave he had seen in a dream, with a stream running in front of it and a Sage standing in the entrance. It could only be Virupaksha. Narasimhayya now told him about Sri Bhagavan. Humphreys was introduced to Ganapati Sastri and conceived great respect for him, and the same month, November 1911, all three of them set out on a visit to Tiruvannamalai.

Humphreys' first impression of the terrific silence of Sri Bhagavan has been quoted already in an earlier chapter. In the same letter from which it is taken he also wrote: "The most touching sight was the number of tiny children, up to about seven years of age, who climb the hill all on their own to come and sit near the Maharshi, even though he may not speak a word nor even look at them for days together. They do not play but just sit there quietly, in perfect contentment."

Like Ganapati Sastri, Humphreys was eager to help the world.

H: Master, can I help the world?

B: Help yourself and you will help the world.

H: I wish to help the world. Shall I not be helpful?

B: Yes, helping yourself you help the world. You are in the world, you are the world. You are not different from the world, nor is the world different from you.

H: (after a pause) Master, can I perform miracles as Sri Krishna and Jesus did before?

B: Did any of them, when he performed them, feel that it was he who was performing a miracle?

H: No, Master.

It was not long before Humphreys repeated his visit.

"I went by motorcycle and climbed up to the cave. The Sage smiled when he saw me but was not in the least surprised. We went in and before we sat down he asked me a question private to myself, of which he knew. Evidently he recognised me the moment he had seen me. Everyone who comes to him is an open book, and a single glance suffices to reveal to him its contents.

'You have not yet had any food,' he said, 'and are hungry.'

"I admitted that it was so and he immediately called in a *chela* (disciple) to bring me food — rice, ghee, fruit, etc., eaten with the fingers, as Indians do not use spoons. Though I have practised eating this way I lack dexterity. So he gave me a coconut spoon to eat with, smiling and talking between whiles. You can imagine nothing more beautiful than his smile. I had coconut milk to drink, whitish, like cow's milk, and delicious, to which he had himself added a few grains of sugar.

"When I had finished I was still hungry and he knew it and ordered more. He knows everything, and when others pressed me to eat fruit when I had had enough he stopped them at once.

"I had to apologise for my way of drinking. He only said, 'Never mind'. The Hindus are particular about this. They never sip nor touch the vessel with their lips but pour the liquid straight in. Thus many can drink from the same cup without fear of infection.

"Whilst I was eating he was relating my past history to others, and accurately too. Yet he had seen me but once before and many hundreds in between. He simply turned on, as it were, clairvoyance, even as we would refer to an encyclopaedia. I sat for about three hours listening to his teaching.

"Later on I was thirsty, for it had been a hot ride, but I would not have shown it for worlds. Yet he knew and told a *chela* to bring me some lemonade.

"At last I had to go, so bowed, as we do, and went outside the cave to put on my boots. He came outside too and said I might come to see him again.

"It is strange what a change it makes in one to have been in his Presence!"

There is no doubt that anyone who sat before Sri Bhagavan was an open book to him; nevertheless Humphreys was probably wrong about the clairvoyance. Although Sri Bhagavan saw through people in order to help and guide them, he did not use any such powers on the human plane. His memory for faces was as phenomenal as for books. Of all the thousands who came, he never forgot a devotee who had once visited him. Even though one returned years later he would be recognised. Nor did he forget the life story of a devotee, and Narasimhayya must have spoken to him about Humphreys. When any matter was best not talked about he showed the utmost discretion, but in general he had the simplicity and disingenuousness of a child and, like a child, would talk about somebody before his face, quite unembarrassed and without causing embarrassment. As for the food and drink, Sri Bhagavan was not only considerate but incredibly observant and would see whether a guest was satisfied.

Thaumaturgic powers began to manifest themselves in Humphreys, but Sri Bhagavan warned him not to indulge them, and he was strong enough to resist the temptation. Indeed, under the influence of Sri Bhagavan, he soon lost all his interest in the occult.

Moreover, he outgrew the fallacy, almost universal in the West and increasingly common in the modern East, that it is possible to help mankind only by outer activity. He had been told that by helping oneself one helps the world; this dictum which the *laissez faire* school falsely supposed to be true economically is in fact true spiritually, since spiritually the wealth of one does not detract from that of others but increases it. Just as he had seen Sri Bhagavan at his very first meeting as a "motionless corpse from which God is radiating terrifically," so everyone, according to his capacity, is a broadcasting station of invisible influences. Insofar as anyone is in a state of harmony and free from egoism he is inevitably and involuntarily emitting harmony, whether he is outwardly active or not; and insofar as his own nature is turbulent and his ego strong he is emitting disharmony even though he may outwardly be performing service.

Although Humphreys never stayed with Sri Bhagavan and only visited him a few times, he imbibed his teaching and received his Grace. A synopsis that he sent to a friend in English was published later in the *International Psychic Gazette* and remains an excellent presentation of the teaching.

"A Master is one who has meditated solely on God, has flung his whole personality into the sea of God, and drowned and forgotten it there, till he becomes only the instrument of God, and when his mouth opens it speaks God's words without effort or forethought; and when he raises a hand, God flows again through that, to work a miracle.

"Do not think too much of psychical phenomena and such things. Their number is legion; and once faith in the psychical thing is established in the heart of a seeker, such phenomena have done their work. Clairvoyance, clairaudience, and such things are not worth having, when so much far greater illumination and peace are possible without them than with them. The Master takes on these powers as a form of self-sacrifice!

"The idea that a Master is simply one who has attained power over the various occult senses by long practice and prayer or anything of the kind, is absolutely false. No Master ever cared a rap for occult powers, for he has no need for them in his daily life.

"The phenomena we see are curious and surprising — but the most marvellous of all we do not realize, and that is that one, and only one illimitable force is responsible for:

(a) All the phenomena we see; and

(b) The act of seeing them.

"Do not fix your attention on all these changing things of life, death and phenomena. Do not think of even the actual act of seeing or perceiving them, but only of that which sees all these things — that which is responsible for it all. This will seem nearly impossible at first, but by degrees the result will be felt. It takes years of steady, daily practice, and that is how a Master is made. Give a quarter of an hour a day for this practice. Try to keep the mind unshakenly fixed on That which sees. It is inside yourself. Do not expect to find that 'That' is something definite on which the mind can be fixed easily; it will not be so. Though it takes years to find that 'That', the result of this concentration will be seen in four or five months' time — in all sorts of unconscious clairvoyance, in peace of mind, in power to deal with troubles, in power all round, yet always unconscious power.[1]

---

[1] Whether in powers or not depend on a man's *prarabdha* (destiny). They are not signs of progress nor their absence of lack of progress.

"I have given you this teaching in the same words as the Master gives to intimate *chelas*. From now onwards, let your whole thought in meditation be not on the act of seeing, nor on what you see, but immovably on That which Sees.

"One gets no reward for Attainment. Then one understands that one does not want a reward. As Krishna says, 'Ye have the right to work, but not to the fruits thereof.' Perfect attainment is simply worship, and worship is attainment.

"If you sit down and realize that you think only by virtue of the one Life, and that the mind, animated by the one Life into the act of thinking, is a part of the whole which is God, then you argue your mind out of existence as a separate entity; and the result is that mind and body, physically (so to speak) disappear; and the only thing that remains is Be-ing, which is at once existence and non-existence and not explainable in words or ideas.

"A Master cannot help being perpetually in this state with only this difference, that in some, to us incomprehensible, way he can use the mind, body and intellect too, without falling back into the delusion of having separate consciousness.

"It is useless to speculate, useless to try and take a mental or intellectual grasp and work from that. That is only religion, a code for children and for social life, a guide to help us to avoid shocks, so that the inside fire may burn up the nonsense in us, and teach us, a little sooner, common sense, *i.e.* a knowledge of the delusion of separateness.

"Religion, whether it be Christianity, Buddhism, Hinduism, Theosophy, or any other kind of 'ism' or 'sophy' or system, can only take us to the one point where all religions meet and no further.

"That one point where all religions meet is the realization — in no mystical sense, but in the most worldly and everyday sense, and the more worldly and everyday and practical the better — of the fact that God is everything, and everything is God.

"From this point begins the work of the practice of this mental comprehension, and all it amounts to is the breaking of a habit. One has to cease calling things 'things', and must call them God; and instead of thinking them to be things, must know them to be God; instead of imagining 'existence' to be the only thing possible, one must realize that this (phenomenal) existence is only the creation of the mind, that 'non-existence' is a necessary sequence if you are going to postulate 'existence'.

"The knowledge of things only shows the existence of an organ to cognize. There are no sounds to the deaf, no sights for the blind, and the mind is merely an organ of conception or of appreciation of certain sides of God.

"God is infinite, and therefore existence and non-existence are merely His counterparts. Not that I wish to say that God is made up of *definite* component parts. It is hard to be comprehensive when talking of God. True knowledge comes from within and not from without. And true knowledge is not 'knowing' but 'seeing'.

"Realization is nothing but seeing God literally. Our greatest mistake is that we think of God as acting symbolically and allegorically, instead of practically and literally.

"Take a piece of glass, paint colours and forms on it, and put the same into a magic lantern, turn on a little

light, and the colours and the forms painted on the glass
are reproduced on the screen. If that light were not turned
on, you would not see the colours of the slide on the screen.

"How are colours formed? By breaking up white light
with a many-sided prism. So it is with a man's character. It
is seen when the Light of Life (God) is shining through it,
i.e. in a man's actions. If the man is sleeping or dead, you
do not see his character. Only when the Light of Life is
animating the character and causing it to act in a thousand
different ways, in response to its contact with this many-
sided world, can you perceive a man's character. If white
light had not been broken up and put into forms and shapes
on our magic lantern slide, we should never have known
that there was a piece of glass in front of the light, for the
light would have shone clearly through. In a sense that
white light was marred, and had some of its clearness taken
from it by having to shine through the colours on the glass.

"So it is with an ordinary man. His mind is like the
screen. On it shines light, dulled and changed because he
has allowed the many-sided world to stand in the way of
the Light (God) and broken it up. He sees only the effects
of the Light (God) instead of the Light (God) Himself,
and his mind reflects the effects he sees just as the screen
reflects the colours on the glass. Take away the prism and
the colours vanish, absorbed back into the white light from
whence they came. Take away the colours from the slide
and the light shines clearly through. Take away from our
sight the world of effects we see, and let us look only into
the cause, and we shall see the Light (God).

"A Master in meditation, though the eyes and ears be
open, fixes his attention so firmly on 'That which sees'

that he neither sees nor hears, nor has any physical consciousness at all — nor mental either, but only spiritual.

"We must take away the world, which causes our doubts, which clouds our mind, and the light of God will shine clearly through. How is the world taken away? When, for example, instead of seeing a man you see and say, 'This is God animating a body', which body answers, more or less perfectly, to the directions of God, as a ship answers more or less perfectly to her helm.

"What are sins? Why, for example, does a man drink too much? Because he hates the idea of being bound — bound by the incapacity to drink as much as he wishes. He is striving after liberty in every sin he commits. This striving after liberty is the first instinctive action of God in a man's mind. For God knows that he is not bound. Drinking too much does not give a man liberty, but then the man does not know that he is really seeking liberty. When he realizes that, he sets about seeking the best way to obtain liberty.

"But the man only gains that liberty when he realizes that he was never bound. The I, I, I's who feel so bound are really the illimitable Spirit. I am bound because I know nothing that I do not sense by one of the senses. Whereas I am all the time that which senses in every body in every mind. These bodies and minds are only the tools of the 'I', the illimitable Spirit.

"What do I want with the tools who am the tools themselves, as the colours are the White Light?"

Needless to say, police service did not prove congenial to Humphreys. Sri Bhagavan advised him to attend to his service and meditation at the same time. For some years he did so and then he retired. Being already a Catholic and having understood the essential unanimity of all the religions, he saw no need to change but returned to England, where he entered a monastery.

RAGHAVACHARIAR

One was often impressed by the tolerance and kindliness of Sri Bhagavan. It was not merely that he recognised the truth of all religions, for that any man of spiritual understanding would do, but if any school or group or ashram was striving to spread spirituality he would show appreciation of the good it was doing, however far its methods might be from his own or its teachings from strict orthodoxy.

Raghavachariar, a government official at Tiruvannamalai, used to visit Sri Bhagavan occasionally. He wanted to ask his opinion of the Theosophical Society but whenever he went he found a crowd of devotees there and he shrank from speaking before them. One day he went determined to submit three questions. This is how he tells of it:

"The questions were:

"1. Can you grant me a few minutes for private, personal talk, free from all others?

"2. I should like to have your opinion of the Theosophical Society, of which I am a member.

"3. Will you please enable me to see your real form if I am eligible to see it.

"When I went and prostrated and sat in his Presence there was a crowd of not less than thirty persons, but one and all they soon dispersed. So I was alone with him and my first query was thus answered without my stating it. That struck me as noteworthy.

"Then he asked me of his own accord if the book in my hand was the *Gita*, and if I was a member of the Theosophical Society and remarked, even before I answered his questions, 'It is doing good work.' I answered his questions in the affirmative.

"My second question also being thus anticipated, I waited with eager mind for the third. After half an hour I opened my mouth and said, 'Just as Arjuna wished to see the form of Sri Krishna and asked for *darshan* (vision of him), I wish to have a *darshan* of your real form, if I am eligible.' He was then seated on the *pial* (dais) with a picture of Dakshinamurti painted on the wall next to him. He silently gazed on, as usual, and I gazed into his eyes. Then his body and also the picture of Dakshinamurti disappeared from my view. There was only empty space, without even a wall, before my eyes. Then a whitish cloud in the outline of the Maharshi and of Dakshinamurti formed before my eyes. Gradually the outline (with silvery lines) of these figures appeared. Then eyes, nose, etc., other details were outlined in lightning-like lines. These gradually broadened till the whole figure of the Sage and Dakshinamurti became ablaze with very strong and unendurable light. I closed my eyes in consequence. I waited for a few minutes and then saw him and Dakshinamurti in the usual form. I prostrated and came away. For a month thereafter I did not dare to go near him, so great was the impression that the above experience made on me. After a month I went up and saw him standing in front of Skandashram. I told him: 'I put a question to you a month back and I had this experience,' narrating the above experience to him. I requested him to explain it. Then, after a pause, he said: 'You wanted to see my form; you saw my disappearance; I am formless. So that experience might be the real truth. The further visions may be according to your own conceptions derived from the study of the *Bhagavad Gita*. But Ganapati Sastri had a similar experience; you may consult him.' I did not in fact consult Sastri. After this Maharshi said, 'Find out who the "I" is, the seer or thinker, and his abode'."

AN ANONYMOUS DEVOTEE

A visitor came to Virupaksha, and although he stayed only five days he so obviously had the Grace of Sri Bhagavan that Narasimhaswami, who was collecting material for the biography, *Self-Realization*, on which a great part of the present work is based, made a point of noting his name and address. There was an elation, a serenity about him, and the radiant eyes of Sri Bhagavan shone on him. Each day he composed a Tamil song in praise of Sri Bhagavan so ecstatic, so spontaneous, so overflowing with joy and devotion, that among all the songs composed, these are of the few that have continued to be sung. Later Narasimhaswami visited Satyamangalam, the town he had named, to collect more particulars about him, but no such person was known there. It has been pointed out that the name means 'Abode of Blessedness' and suggested that the visitor may have been an emissary from some hidden 'Abode of Blessedness' come to pay homage to the Sadguru of the age.

One of his songs hails Sri Bhagavan as 'Ramana Sadguru'. Once when it was being sung Sri Bhagavan himself joined in. The devotee who was singing it laughed and said, "This is the first time I have heard anyone singing his own praise."

Sri Bhagavan replied, "Why limit Ramana to these six feet? Ramana is universal."

One of the five songs is so instinct with the joys of dawn and awakening that one can well believe it may have celebrated the true dawn for him who composed it:

> Dawn is rising on the Hill,
> Sweet Ramana, come!
> Lord Arunachala, come!
>
> In the bush the koel sings,
> Dear Master, Ramana, come!
> Lord of Knowledge, come!
>
> The conch blows, the stars are dim.
> Sweet Ramana, come!
> Lord God of Gods, come!
>
> The cocks crow, the birds chirp,
> It is already time, come!
> The night has fled, come!
>
> The trumpets blow, the drums beat
> Gold-bright Ramana, come!
> Knowledge Awake, come!
>
> The crows caw, it is morn,
> Snake-decked Lord, come![1]
> Blue-throated Lord, come![1]
>
> Ignorance is fled, the lotuses[2] open,
> Wise Lord Ramana, come!
> Crown of the Vedas, come!

---

[1] An epithet of Siva.

[2] This implies also 'the hearts'.

Unstained by qualities, Lord of Liberation,
Gracious Ramana, come!
Lord Peace, come!

Sage and Lord,
One with Being-Knowledge-Bliss,
Lord dancing in joy,[1] come!

Love on the summit of Knowledge,
Past pleasure, past pain, come!
Blissful Silence, come!

---

[1] An epithet of Siva.

11
ANIMALS

IT IS HELD in Hinduism (as expounded, for instance, by Shankaracharya in his commentary on the *Bhagavad Gita*, Ch. V, vv. 40-44) that after death one who has not dissolved the illusion of a separate individuality in realization of identity with the Self passes on to a state of heaven or hell according to the good or bad karma or balance-sheet he has accumulated during his earth-life, and that, after the exhaustion of this harvest-time, he again returns to earth, to a high or low birth in conformity with his karma, in order to work out that part of it known as *prarabdha*, that is to say the destiny of one lifetime. During his new earth-life he again accumulates *agamya* or new karma, and this is added on to his *sanchitha*-karma or that residue of his already accumulated karma which is not *prarabdha*.

It is commonly held that progress can be made and karma worked off only during a human life; however Sri Bhagavan has indicated that it is possible for animals also to be working off their karma. In a conversation quoted in this chapter he said, "We do not know what souls may be tenanting these bodies and for finishing what part of their unfinished karma they may seek our company." Shankaracharya also affirmed that animals can attain Liberation. Moreover, one of the Puranas tells how the Sage Jada-Bharata was assailed while dying by a fleeting thought of his tame deer and had to be born again as a deer in order to exorcise this last remaining attachment.

Sri Bhagavan showed the same consideration to the animals whom destiny had brought into contact with him as to the people. And animals were no less attracted to him than people. Already at Gurumurtam birds and squirrels used to build their nests around him. In those days devotees supposed that he was as oblivious to the world as he was unattached to it, but in fact he was keenly observant and he has since told of a squirrel family that occupied a nest abandoned there by some birds.

He never referred to an animal in the normal Tamil style as 'it' but always as 'he' or 'she'. "Have the lads been given their food?" — and it would be the Ashram dogs he was referring to. "Give Lakshmi her rice at once" — and it was the cow Lakshmi that he meant. It was a regular Ashram rule that at meal-time the dogs were fed first, then any beggars who came, and last the devotees. Knowing Sri Bhagavan's reluctance to accept anything that is not shared by all alike, I was surprised once to see him tasting a mango between meals, and then I saw the reason — the mango season was just beginning and he wanted to see whether it was ripe enough to give to the white peacock that had been sent from the Maharani of Baroda and had become his ward. There were other peacocks also. He would call to them, imitating their cry, and they would come to him and receive peanuts, rice, mango. On the last day before his physical death, when the doctors said the pain must be frightful, he heard a peacock screech on a nearby tree and asked whether they had received their food.

Squirrels used to hop through the window on to his couch and he would always keep a little tin of peanuts beside him for them. Sometimes he would hand a visiting squirrel the tin and let it help itself; sometimes he would hold out a nut and the little creature would take it from his hand. One day, when, on account of his age and rheumatism, he had begun to walk with the aid of a staff, he was descending the few steps into the Ashram compound when a squirrel ran past his feet, chased by a dog. He called out to the dog and threw his staff between them, and in doing so he slipped and broke his collar-bone; but the dog was distracted and the squirrel saved.

The animals felt his Grace. If a wild animal is cared for by people its own kind boycott it on its return to them, but if it came from him they did not; rather they seemed to honour it. They felt the complete absence of fear and anger in him. He was sitting on the hillside when a snake crawled over his legs. He neither moved nor showed any alarm. A devotee asked him what it felt like to have a snake pass over one and, laughing he replied "Cool and soft."

He would not have snakes killed where he resided. "We have come to their home and have no right to trouble or disturb them. They do not molest us." And they didn't. Once his mother was frightened when a cobra approached her. Sri Bhagavan walked towards it and it turned and went away. It passed between two rocks and he followed it; however, the passage ended against a rock-wall and, being unable to escape, it turned and coiled its body and looked at him. He also looked. This continued for some minutes and then the cobra uncoiled and, feeling no more need for fear, crawled quietly away, passing quite close to his feet.

Once when he was sitting with some devotees at Skandashram a mongoose ran up to him and sat for awhile on his lap. "Who knows why it came?" he said. "It could have been no ordinary mongoose." There is another case of a far from ordinary mongoose told by Professor Venkatramiah in his diary. In answer to a question by Mr. Grant Duff, Sri Bhagavan said:

"It was on the occasion of *Arudra Darshan* (a Saivite festival). I was then living on the Hill at Skandashram. Streams of visitors were climbing up the Hill from the town and a mongoose, uncommonly large and of a golden hue, not the usual grey colour, and without the usual black spot on its tail, passed fearlessly through the crowds. People thought it was a tame one and that its owner must be among the crowd. It went straight up to Palaniswami, who was taking a bath in the spring by Virupaksha Cave. He stroked the creature and patted it. It followed him into the cave, inspected every nook and corner of it, and then joined the crowd to pass up to Skandashram. Everyone was struck by its attractive appearance and fearless movements. It came to me, climbed on to my lap, and rested there for some time. Then it raised itself up, looked around and moved down. It went around the whole place and I followed it lest it should be harmed by careless visitors or by the peacocks. Two peacocks did look at it inquisitively, but it moved calmly from place to place until finally it disappeared among the rocks to the south-east of the Ashram."

Once Sri Bhagavan was cutting up vegetables for the Ashram kitchen in the early morning before sunrise, together with two devotees. One of them, Lakshmana Sharma, had brought his dog with him — a handsome, pure white dog — and it was dashing about in high spirits and refused the food offered to it. Sri Bhagavan said: "You see what joy he shows? He is a high soul who has taken on this canine form."

Professor Venkatramiah has told in his diary of a remarkable case of devotion in the Ashram dogs:

> "At that time (*i.e.* in 1924) there were four dogs in the Ashram. Sri Bhagavan said that they would not accept any food unless he himself had partaken of it. The pandit put this to the test by spreading some food before them, but they would not touch it. After awhile Sri Bhagavan put a morsel of it into his mouth and immediately they fell upon it and devoured it."

The ancestress of most of the Ashram dogs was Kamala, who came to Skandashram as a puppy. The devotees tried to drive her away, fearing that she would litter the Ashram with pups year after year, but she refused to go. A large canine family did indeed grow up, but they all had to be treated with equal consideration. On the occasion of her first delivery, Kamala was given her bath, painted with turmeric, decked with vermilion on the forehead and given a clean place in the Ashram where she remained for ten days with her pups. And on the tenth day her purification was celebrated with regular feasting. She was an intelligent and serviceable dog. Sri Bhagavan would often depute her to take a newcomer round the Hill. "Kamala, take this stranger round"; and she would guide him to every image, tank and shrine around the hill.

One of the most remarkable of the dogs, though not of Kamala's progeny, was Chinna Karuppan (Little Blackie). Sri Bhagavan himself has given an account of him. "Chinna Karuppan was pure black all over, whence his name. He was a person of high principles. When we were in Virupaksha Cave something black used to pass us at a distance. We would sometimes see his head peeping over the bushes. His *vairagya* (dispassion) seemed to be very strong. He kept company with none, and in fact seemed to avoid company. We respected his independence and *vairagya* and used to leave food near his place and go away. One day, as we were going up, Karuppan suddenly jumped across the path and romped upon me, wagging his tail in glee. How he singled me out from the group for his display of affection was the wonder. Thereafter he remained with us in the Ashram as one of the inmates. A very intelligent and serviceable fellow he was, and how high-minded! He had lost all his former aloofness and became very affectionate. It was a case of universal brotherhood. He would make friends with every visitor and inmate, climb on to his lap and nestle against him. His overtures were generally well received. A few tried to avoid him but he was indefatigable in his efforts and would take no refusal as final. However, if he was ordered away he would obey like a monk observing the vow of obedience. Once he went near an orthodox Brahmin who was reciting mantras at the foot of a bel-tree near our cave. The Brahmin regarded dogs as unclean and scrupulously avoided contact or even proximity to them. However, Karuppan, evidently understanding and observing only the natural law of equality (*samatvam*), insisted on going near him. Out of consideration for the Brahmin's feelings an inmate of the Ashram raised his stick and beat the dog, though not hard. Karuppan wailed and ran away and never returned to the

Ashram, nor was seen again. He would never again approach a place where he had been once ill-treated, so sensitive he was.

"The person who made this mistake evidently underrated the dog's principles and sensitivity. And yet there had already been a warning. It was like this. Palaniswami had once spoken and behaved rudely to Chinna Karuppan. It was a cold, rainy night, but all the same Chinna Karuppan left the premises and spent the whole night on a bag of charcoal some distance away. It was only in the morning that he was brought back. There had also been a warning from the behaviour of another dog. Some years back Palaniswami scolded a small dog that was with us at Virupaksha Cave and the dog ran straight down to Sankhatirtham Tank and soon after his dead body was floating there. Palaniswami and all the others at the Ashram were at once told that dogs and other animal inmates of the Ashram have intelligence and principles of their own and should not be treated roughly. We do not know what souls may be tenanting these bodies and for finishing what portion of their unfinished karma they may seek our company."

There were other dogs also that showed intelligence and high principles. While at Skandashram, Sri Bhagavan was usually beside one of the Ashram dogs when it breathed its last and the body was given a decent burial and a stone placed over the grave. In the later years, when the Ashram buildings had been put up and especially when Sri Bhagavan began to grow less active in body, the humans had it more their own way and animal devotees had little access.

Until the last few years monkeys still came to the window beside Sri Bhagavan's couch and looked in through the bars. Sometimes one saw monkey mothers with the little ones clinging to them, as if to show them to Bhagavan, just as human mothers did. As a sort of compromise, the attendants were allowed to drive them away but were expected to throw them a banana before doing so.

Until he became too infirm, Sri Bhagavan walked on the Hill every morning after seven and every evening at about five o'clock. One evening, instead of the usual short walk, he went up to Skandashram. When he did not return at the usual time, some devotees followed him up the Hillside, others gathered in small clusters, discussing where he had gone, what it meant, and what to do about it, others sat in the hall, waiting. A pair of monkeys came to the hall door and, forgetting their fear of people, stepped inside and looked anxiously at the empty couch.

After that, a few years before humans also lost their sight of Sri Bhagavan on earth, the day of the monkeys was finished. The palm-leaf roofs outside the hall were extended, making access more difficult for them, and anyway most of them were taken back to the jungle or captured by the municipality and sent to America to be experimented on.

From 1900, when Sri Bhagavan first went to live on the Hill, to 1922, when he came down to the Ashram at its foot, he was very intimate with the monkeys. He watched them closely, with the love and sympathy that the *Jnani* (Sage) has for all beings and with that keen observation that was natural to him. He learnt to understand their cries and got to know their code of behaviour and system of government. He discovered that each tribe has its king and its recognised district, and if another tribe infringes on this there will be war. But before starting a war or making peace an ambassador is sent from one tribe to the other. He would tell visitors that he was recognised by the monkeys as one of their community and accepted as arbiter in their disputes.

"Monkeys, as a rule, would boycott one of their group if he had been cared for by people, but they make an exception in my case. Also, when there is misunderstanding and quarrelling they come to me and I pacify them by pushing them apart and so stop their quarrelling. A young monkey was once bitten by an elder member of his group and left helpless near the Ashram. The little fellow came limping to the Ashram at Virupaksha Cave, hence we called him Nondi (the Lame). When his group came along five days later they saw that he was tended by me but still they took him back. From then on they would all come to get any little thing that could be spared for them outside the Ashram, but Nondi would come right on to my lap. He was a scrupulously clean eater. When a leaf-plate of rice was set before him he would not spill a single grain of rice outside it. If he ever did spill any he would pick it up and eat it before going on with what was on the plate.

"He was very sensitive though. Once, for some reason, he threw out some food and I scolded him.... 'What! Why are you wasting food?' He at once hit me over the eye and hurt me slightly. As a punishment he was not allowed to come to me and climb on to my lap for some days, but the little fellow cringed and begged hard and regained his happy seat. That was his second offence. On the first occasion I put his cup of hot milk to my lips to blow it, so as to cool it for him, and he was annoyed and hit me over the eye, but there was no serious hurt and he at once came back to my lap and cringed as though to say, 'Forget and forgive', so he was excused."

Later on Nondi became king of his tribe. Sri Bhagavan also told of another monkey king who took the bold step of outlawing two turbulent males in his tribe. The tribe thereupon became restive and the king left them and went alone into the jungle where he remained for two weeks. When he returned he challenged the critics and rebels, and so strong had he become through his two weeks *tapas* (privation) that none dared answer his challenge.

Early one morning it was reported that a monkey lay dying near the Ashram. Sri Bhagavan went to see and it was this king. It was brought to the Ashram and lay supporting itself against Sri Bhagavan. The two exiled males were sitting on a tree nearby, watching. Sri Bhagavan moved to shift his weight and the dying monkey instinctively bit his leg. "I have four such marks of favour from monkey kings," he said once, pointing to his leg. Then the monkey king uttered a last groan as he expired. The two watching monkeys jumped up and down and cried out with grief. The body was buried with the honours given to a *sanyasin*: it was bathed in milk and then in water and smeared with sacred ashes; a new cloth was placed over it leaving the face uncovered and camphor burnt before it. It was given a grave near the Ashram and over this a stone was raised.

One strange story of monkey gratitude is told. Sri Bhagavan was once walking round the foot of the Hill with a group of devotees and when they got near Pachaiamman Koil they felt hungry and thirsty. Immediately a tribe of monkeys climbed the wild fig trees at the roadside and shook the branches, strewing the road with the ripe fruit, and then ran away, not eating any themselves. And at the same time a group of women came up with earthen jars of water for drinking.

The most favoured of all the animal devotees of Sri Bhagavan was the cow Lakshmi. She was brought to the Ashram as a young calf together with her mother in 1926 by one Arunachala Pillai of Kumaramangalam near Gudiyatham and presented to Sri Bhagavan. He was reluctant to accept the gift as there was then no accommodation for cows at the Ashram. However, Arunachala Pillai absolutely refused to take them back and a devotee, Ramanath Dikshitar, offered to look after them, so they stayed. Dikshitar saw to their needs for about three months and then they were left with someone in town who kept cows. He kept them for about a year and then one day came to have *darshan* of Sri Bhagavan and brought them with him on a visit. The calf seems to have been irresistibly attracted to Sri Bhagavan and to have noted the way to the Ashram because she returned alone next day and from then on came every morning and returned to town only in the evening. Later, when she came to live in the Ashram, she would still come to Sri Bhagavan, going straight up to him and taking no notice of anyone else, and Sri Bhagavan would always have bananas or some other delicacy for her. For a long time she would come to the hall daily at lunchtime to accompany him to the dining hall, and so punctually that if he had been occupied by anything and sat beyond the hour he would look at the clock when she came in and find that it was time.

She bore a number of calves, at least three of them on Bhagavan's *Jayanthi* (birthday). When a stone cow-house was built in the Ashram it was decided that Lakshmi should be the first to enter it on the day of its inauguration, but when the time came she could not be found; she had gone to lie by Sri Bhagavan and would not budge until he came too, so that he entered first and she behind him. Not only was she uncommonly devoted to Sri Bhagavan, but the Grace and kindness he showed her was quite exceptional. In later years there were a number of cows and bulls at the Ashram but no other that formed such an attachment or elicited such Grace. Lakshmi's descendants are still there.

On June 17th, 1948, Lakshmi fell ill and on the morning of the 18th it seemed that her end was near. At ten o'clock Sri Bhagavan went to her. "Amma (Mother)," he said, "you want me to be near you?" He sat down beside her and took her head on his lap. He gazed into her eyes and placed his hand on her head as though giving her *diksha* (initiation) and also over her heart. Holding his cheek against hers, he caressed her. Satisfied that her heart was pure and free from all *vasanas* (latent tendencies) and centred wholly on Bhagavan, he took leave of her and went to the dining hall for lunch. Lakshmi was conscious up to the end; her eyes were calm. At eleven-thirty she left her body, quite peacefully. She was buried in the Ashram compound with full funeral rites, beside the graves of a deer, a crow and a dog which Sri Bhagavan had also caused to be buried there. A square stone was placed over her grave surmounted by a likeness of her. On the stone was engraved an epitaph that Sri Bhagavan had written stating that she had attained *Mukti* (Liberation). Devaraja Mudaliar asked Bhagavan whether that was used as a conventional phrase, as the phrase that someone has attained *samadhi* is a polite way of saying that he has died, or whether it really meant *Mukti*, and Sri Bhagavan said that it meant *Mukti*.

12

SRI RAMANASHRAM

WHEN THE DEVOTEES followed Sri Bhagavan down to the Mother's *samadhi* at the foot of the Hill in December 1922 there was only a single thatched shed for Ashram. Through the ensuing years the numbers grew, donations came in and regular Ashram premises were erected — the hall where Sri Bhagavan sat, the office and bookshop, the dining hall and kitchen, the cowshed, the post office, the dispensary, the guest-room for male visitors (really not a room but a large dormitory for such as wished to stay some days at the Ashram), a couple of small bungalows for guests who made a longer stay — all single-storey buildings whitewashed on the outside in Indian fashion.

Immediately to the west of the Ashram is a large square tank with stone steps leading down to the water from all four

sides. South of the Ashram the bus road from Tiruvannamalai
to Bangalore runs east and west, the road which bifurcates farther
west and swings round to circle the Hill. As one stands on the
road, facing northwards, one sees, across a small culvert, a
wooden arch painted black with the name 'Sri Ramanasramam'[1]
in gold lettering. No gate, just an open approach. [2] The fronds
of coconut palms screen the Ashram buildings and beyond them,
imminent, majestic, rises the Hill.

Nor was it only the Ashram itself that was built. Across the
road the Maharaja of Morvi endowed a guest house for visiting
rajahs. A colony of cottages and bungalows sprang up, built by
the householder devotees. Immediately west of the Ashram,
between the tank and the Hill, sadhus made a colony at
Palakottu, living in caves or huts among the trees. In the Ashram
itself such as were drawn more to action than meditation lived a
life of service in the office, the garden, the bookstall, the kitchen,
one department or other, counting themselves blessed to be near
Sri Bhagavan, to see him pass, perhaps occasionally to be noticed,
to be spoken to by him.

All this building and planning and the handling of money
required an Ashram management because Sri Bhagavan would
do none of these things. Therefore his brother, Niranjanananda
Swami, became the *Sarvardhikari* or Ruler of the Ashram.
Regulations grew up governing Ashram life. Some of them were
irksome to the devotees; however, if any felt tempted to protest
or revolt the attitude of Sri Bhagavan restrained them, for he
submitted to every rule and upheld authority, not so much
perhaps, on the particular issue at stake as on the general ground

---

[1] The forms 'ashram' and 'asramam' are both correct, one corresponding to
the Sanskrit and the other to the Tamil.

[2] This has now changed.

that orders should be obeyed. There was significance in this, as in all he did.

He was enjoining a path that is to be followed not in isolation but in the conditions of the world in this *kaliyuga*, this spiritually dark age, and if he urged his followers to remember the Self while submitting to conditions that might not be congenial, he himself set the example by conforming to all the Ashram rules. Moreover, he disapproved of people turning aside from the purpose for which they had approached him to engage in disputes of management. He said, "People walk up the drive to the Ashram in search of Deliverance and then get caught up in Ashram politics and forget what they came for." If such matters were their concern they need not have come to Tiruvannamalai for them.

There were occasional outbursts of opposition and discontent, and one cannot say that they were altogether unjustified on the actual merits of the case, but Sri Bhagavan did not countenance them. Once a group of devotees, business and professional men from Madras, came in a specially chartered bus to demand the total removal of the Ashram management and the institution of a new system. They trooped into the hall and sat down before Sri Bhagavan. He sat silent, his face hard, aloof, eternal as rock. They grew uneasy before him, glanced at one another, shuffled and not one of them presumed to speak. Finally they left the hall and returned to Madras as they had come. Only then Sri Bhagavan was told what their errand had been, and he said: "I wonder what they come here for. Do they come to reform themselves or to reform the Ashram?"

At the same time — another lesson that had to be observed — if any rule appeared not merely irksome but unjust he would not submit to it, just as he did not submit to the levy of a fee at Virupaksha Cave. Even then, his method was seldom actually to protest but rather to draw attention to the injustice by his behaviour. There was a time when meals were already served in the Ashram dining hall but it was not found possible to provide proper coffee for all, so those of less consequence, who ate farthest away at the end of the hall, were given water. Sri Bhagavan noticed — he always noticed everything — and said, "Give me water too." After that he drank water and never accepted coffee again.

Once when he was already advanced in age and his knees stiff and deformed with rheumatism, a party of Europeans came; one lady among them, being unaccustomed to sit cross-legged, leaned against the wall and stretched her legs out in front of her. An attendant, perhaps not realizing how painful it is to sit cross-legged for one not used to it, told her not to sit like that. The poor lady flushed with embarrassment and drew in her legs. Sri Bhagavan immediately sat upright and cross-legged. Despite the pain in his knees he continued so and when the devotees asked him not to, he said: "If that is the rule I must obey it as well as anyone else. If it is disrespectful to stretch out one's feet I am being disrespectful to every person in the hall." The attendant had already left the hall but was brought back and asked the lady to sit as was most convenient. Even then it was difficult to persuade Sri Bhagavan to relax.

In the early years criticism was sometimes encountered. Western devotees in particular were subject to missionary onslaughts. One enthusiast even entered the hall and launched his rhetoric at Sri Bhagavan himself. Sri Bhagavan did not reply, but Major Chadwick's voice booming out a challenge from the back of the hall to the speaker's interpretation of Christianity, so disconcerted him that he gave up the attempt. Even in later years Catholic priests continued to come, to show interest and reverence and then to throw out some doubt in a way that made one wonder whether their hearts were open or whether their purpose was not merely proselytism and misrepresentation.

A Muslim came once to argue, but there must have been sincerity behind his challenge because Sri Bhagavan answered it patiently.

"Has God a form?" he asked.

"Who says God has a form?" Sri Bhagavan retorted.

The questioner persisted, "If God is formless is it not wrong to ascribe to Him the form of an idol and worship Him in it?"

He had understood the retort to mean, "Nobody says God has a form." But it meant exactly what it said and was now amplified, "Let God alone; tell me first whether *you* have a form."

"Of course I have a form, as you can see, but I am not God."

"Are you then the physical body made of flesh and bones and blood and nicely dressed?"

"Yes, that must be so; I am aware of my existence in this bodily form."

"You call yourself that body because now you are aware of your body, but are you that body? Can it be yourself in deep sleep when you are quite unaware of its existence?"

"Yes, I must have remained in the same bodily form even in deep sleep because I am aware of it until I fall asleep, and as soon as I wake I see that I am just as I was when I went to sleep."

"And when death occurs?"

The questioner stopped and thought a minute, "Well, then I am considered dead and the body is buried."

"But you said your body is yourself. When it is being taken away to be buried why doesn't it protest and say: 'No! no! don't take me away! This property I have acquired, these clothes I am wearing, these children I have begotten, they are all mine, I must remain with them'!"

The visitor then confessed that he had wrongly identified himself with the body and said, "I am the life in the body, not the body in itself."

Then Sri Bhagavan explained to him: "Till now you seriously considered yourself to be the body and to have a form. That is the primal ignorance which is the root cause of all trouble. Until that ignorance is got rid of, until you know your formless nature, it is mere pedantry to argue about God and whether He has a form or is formless or whether it is right to worship God in the form of an idol when He is really formless. Until one sees the formless Self one cannot truly worship the formless God."

Sometimes the answers given were terse and cryptic, sometimes full and explanatory, but always adapted to the questioner and always marvellously apt. A naked fakir came once and stayed for about a week, sitting with his right arm held permanently aloft. He did not come into the hall himself but sent in the question, "What will my future be?"

"Tell him his future will be as his present is," was the reply. Not only did it rebuke this interest in the future, but it reminded him that his present activity, sincere or insincere, was creating his future state.

A visitor made a display of knowledge, rehearsing the different paths presented by various masters and quoting from Western philosophers. "One says one thing and one another," he concluded. "Which of you is right? Which way should I go?"

Sri Bhagavan remained silent, but the visitor persisted in his question, "Please tell me which way I should go."

As Sri Bhagavan rose to leave the hall he replied curtly, "Go the way you came."

The visitor complained to the devotees that the answer was unhelpful, and they pointed out its profounder implications: that the only way is to return to one's Source, to go back whence one came. At the same time, it was just the reply he deserved.

Sundaresa Aiyar, a devotee already referred to, heard that he was to be transferred to another town and complained in his grief: "Forty years I have been with Bhagavan and now I am to be sent away. What shall I do away from Bhagavan?"

"How long have you been with Bhagavan?" he was asked.

"Forty years."

Then, turning to the devotees, Sri Bhagavan said, "Here is someone who has been listening to my teaching for forty years and now says he is going somewhere away from Bhagavan!" Thus did he draw attention to his universal presence. Nevertheless, the transfer was cancelled.

Year after year the little hall remained the centre of the devotees and the focus of all those the world over who could not be physically present. To a superficial observer it might seem that little was happening, but really the activity was tremendous.

Through the years the routine of life changed a little; also more routine, more restrictions, grew up with the gradual weakening of Bhagavan's physical form. Until the frailty of age set in there were no set hours for approaching him. He was accessible at all times, day and night. Even when he slept he would not have the hall doors closed lest any who needed him might be shut out. Often he himself would talk to a group of devotees far into the night. Some of them, like Sundaresa Aiyar, were householders with work to do next day, and they found that after a night spent thus with Sri Bhagavan they felt no fatigue next day from loss of sleep.

In the actual round of daily life at the Ashram there was orderliness and punctuality because this was a part of that acceptance of the conditions of life which Sri Bhagavan exemplified and enjoined. So also, everything was clean and tidy and in its right place.

There was a time when he used to rise very often at about three or four in the morning and spend an hour or two peeling and cutting up vegetables or making leaf-plates (before banana leaves began to be grown at the Ashram and used for eating on). In this, as in everything, devotees would gather round and help, for the pleasure of being near him. Sometimes he would take a hand with the actual cooking. He gave instructions that the vegetable peelings were not to be thrown away but given to the cattle. Nothing was to be wasted. One day he found that, despite his instructions, they had been thrown away, and he never joined in the kitchen work again.

Already in 1926 he gave up making *giri pradakshina* (circuit of the Hill). The crowds were becoming so large as to be unmanageable; none were willing to remain in the Ashram when he went, but all wished to accompany him. Moreover, visitors might come for *darshan* — for his Presence — while he was away and return disappointed at not finding him there. On more than one occasion he indicated that giving *darshan* was, so to speak, his task in life and that he must be accessible to all who came. He mentioned this as one of the reasons for remaining at the foot of the Hill instead of returning to Skandashram, which is less easily accessible. Not only did he give up making *pradakshina*, but he never absented himself from the Ashram for any reason at all, except for a short walk morning and evening.

Even his giving up work in the kitchen was probably due largely to the need to be accessible to all the devotees, since only a few could join him in such work. When he was urged to make a tour of the holy places of India one of the reasons he gave for refusing was that devotees might come to the Ashram and not find him there. And during his last sickness he insisted to the very end that all who came should have *darshan*.

Volumes could be filled with the experiences of devotees during these years and the instructions and expositions they received. However, it is not the purpose of this book to give an exhaustive account, but rather a general picture of the life and teaching of Sri Bhagavan.

13
LIFE WITH SRI BHAGAVAN

IT IS, PERHAPS, harder to visualise the Divine Man in the technique of daily living than in miracle or transfiguration, and for this a description of the routine of life during the last years will be helpful. The incidents that are fitted into it are no more noteworthy than many that went before, just as the devotees referred to are no more outstanding than many who remain unmentioned.

It is 1947 already. Fifty years have passed at Tiruvannamalai. With the onset of age and failing health, restrictions have been imposed and Sri Bhagavan is no longer accessible privately and at all hours. He sleeps on the couch where he gives *darshan*, the blessing of his Presence, during the day, but with closed doors now. At five o'clock the doors open and early morning devotees enter quietly, prostrate themselves before him and sit down on the black stone floor, worn smooth and shiny with use, many of them on small mats they have brought with them. Why did Sri Bhagavan, who was so modest, who insisted on equal treatment with the humblest, allow this prostration before him? Although humanly he refused all privileges, he recognised that adoration of the outwardly manifested Guru was helpful to *sadhana*, to spiritual progress. Not that outward forms of submission were sufficient. He once said explicitly, "Men prostrate themselves before me but I know who is submitted in his heart."

A small group of Brahmins, resident at the Ashram, sit near the head of the couch and intone the Vedas; one or two others who have walked from the town, a mile and a half away, join them. At the foot of the couch incense-sticks are lit, diffusing their subtle perfume through the air. If it is in the winter months a brazier of burning charcoal stands beside the couch, a pathetic reminder of his failing vitality. Sometimes he warms his frail hands and thin tapering fingers, those exquisitely beautiful hands at the glow and rubs a little warmth into his limbs. All sit quietly mostly with eyes closed in meditation.

A few minutes before six the chanting ends. All rise and stand as Sri Bhagavan raises himself with an effort from the couch, reaches out for the staff that the attendant places in his hand, and walks with slow steps to the door. It is not from weakness or fear of falling that he walks with downcast gaze; one feels that it is an innate modesty. He leaves the hall by its north door, on the side of the Hill, and passes slowly, leaning on his staff and a little bent, along the passage between the white-walled dining hall and office building, then, skirting the men's guest house, to the bathroom beside the cowshed, farthest east of the Ashram buildings. Two attendants follow him, stocky, short and dark and wearing white *dhoties* down to the ankles, while he is tall and slim and golden-hued and clad only in a white loincloth. Only occasionally he looks up if some devotee approaches him or to smile upon some child.

There is no way of describing the radiance of his smile. One who might appear a hardened businessman would leave Tiruvannamalai with a lilt in his heart from that smile. A simple woman said: "I don't understand the philosophy but when he smiles at me I feel safe, just like a child in its mother's arms. I had never yet seen him when I received a letter from my five-year-old daughter: 'You will love Bhagavan. When he smiles everyone must be so happy'."

Breakfast is at seven. After breakfast Sri Bhagavan goes for a short walk and then returns to the hall. In the interval it has been swept out and clean covers placed on the couch, some of them richly embroidered, being presents from devotees. All are spotlessly clean and very carefully folded, for the attendants know how observant he is and how every little detail will be noticed, whether it is remarked upon or not.

By eight o'clock Sri Bhagavan is back in the hall and the devotees begin to arrive. By nine the hall is full. If you are a newcomer you probably feel how intimate the hall is, how close you are to the Master, for the entire space is only 40 feet by 15. It runs east and west with a door in each long side. That on the north, facing the Hill, opens out on to a tree-shaded square with the dining hall running along its eastern side and on its west the garden and dispensary. That on the south leads out to the temple and, beyond it, the road, the side from which the devotees arrive. The couch is at the northeast of the hall. Beside it is a revolving bookcase containing the books most frequently in demand, and on it stands a clock, while another hangs on the wall beside the couch, both right to the minute.

If any book is needed for reference Sri Bhagavan will know just where it stands, on which shelf, and probably the very page of the passage to be referred to. Large bookcases with glass-panelled doors stand along the south wall.

Most of the devotees sit in the body of the hall, facing Sri Bhagavan, that is facing east, the women in front of him, down the northern half of the hall, the men to his left. Only a few of the men sit alongside the couch, with their backs to the south wall and nearer to Sri Bhagavan than the others. A few years previously it was the women who had this privilege and then, for some reason, the positions were changed. It is the Hindu tradition for men and women to sit apart and Sri Bhagavan approves of it, as the magnetism between them may disturb the greater spiritual magnetism.

Again the incense sticks are burning. Some there are, now also, who sit with eyes closed in meditation, but others relax and simply feast their eyes on Sri Bhagavan. A visitor sings songs of praise that he has composed. One who has been away and is returning, offers a tribute of fruit at his feet, and then finds a place in the seated ranks before him. An attendant gives back a part of the offering as the grace or *prasadam* of Sri Bhagavan; something may be given to children who enter the hall, to monkeys who stand at the window near the couch or peer round the door, to the peacocks, or to the cow Lakshmi if she pays a visit. The rest is taken later to the dining hall to be shared among the devotees.

Sri Bhagavan accepts nothing for himself. There is an ineffable tenderness in his look. It is not only sympathy for the immediate troubles of his devotees but for the whole vast burden of *samsara*, of human life. And yet, despite the tenderness, the lines of his face can show the sternness of one who has conquered and never compromised. This aspect of hardness is usually covered by a soft growth of white hair, for, as a *sanyasin*, his head and face are shaved every full moon day. Many of the devotees regret it — the growth of white hair on face and head so enhances the grace and gentleness of aspect — but none presumes to mention it to him.

His face is like the face of water, always changing, yet always the same. It is amazing how swiftly it moves from gentleness to rock-like grandeur, from laughter to compassion. So completely does each successive aspect live that one feels it is not one man's face but the face of all mankind. Technically he may not be beautiful, for the features are not regular; and yet the most beautiful face looks trivial beside him. Such reality is in his face that its impress sinks deep in the memory and abides when others fade. Even those who have seen him only for a short time or only in a photograph recall him to their mind's eye more vividly than those they know well. Indeed, it may be that the love, the grace, the wisdom, the deep understanding, the childlike innocence that shines from such a picture is a better starting point for meditation than any words.

Around the couch, a couple of feet away from it, is a movable railing about eighteen inches high. That caused a little controversy at first. The Ashram management observed how Sri Bhagavan normally avoided being touched and drew back if any made to do so. Recollecting, moreover, how a misguided devotee had once broken a coconut and wanted to honour him by pouring the milk over his head, they decided that so much seclusion would be better. Many of the devotees, on the other hand, felt that it was placing a sort of barrier between them and

Sri Bhagavan. The discussion as to whether he approved of this went on in front of him, but none presumed to ask him for a decision. Bhagavan sat unaffected.

Some of the devotees, without rising from their places, talk with Sri Bhagavan about themselves or their friends, give news of absent devotees, ask doctrinal questions. One feels the homely atmosphere, as of a great family. Perhaps someone has a private matter to report and goes up to the couch to speak to Sri Bhagavan in an undertone or to hand him a paper on which he has written it out. It may be that he wants an answer or that it is enough simply to inform Sri Bhagavan and he has faith that all will be well.

A mother brings a little child in and he smiles to it more beautifully than a mother. A little girl brings her doll and makes it prostrate before the couch and then shows it to Bhagavan who takes it and looks at it. A young monkey slips in at the door and tries to grab a banana. The attendant chases it out, but there happens to be only one attendant present, so it runs round the end of the hall and in through the other door and Sri Bhagavan whispers urgently to it: "Hurry! Hurry! He'll be back soon." A wild-looking sadhu with matted locks and ochre robe stands with hands upraised before the couch. A prosperous townsman in a European suit makes a decorous prostration and secures a front seat; his companion, not quite sure of his devotion, does not prostrate at all.

A group of pandits sit near the couch, translating a Sanskrit work, and from time to time take it up to him to elucidate some point. A three-year-old, not to be outdone, takes up his story of Little Bo Peep, and Sri Bhagavan takes that too, just as graciously, and looks through it with the same interest; but it is tattered, so he passes it to an attendant to bind and gives it back next day neatly repaired.

The attendant is painstaking in his work. He needs to be because Sri Bhagavan himself is keen of eye and hand and will pass no slovenly work. The attendants feel that they enjoy the especial Grace of Sri Bhagavan. So do the pandits. So does the three-year-old. One gradually perceives how the profound immediacy of response leads devotees utterly varied in mind and character to feel a special personal intimacy with the Master.

Gradually also one perceives something of the skill and subtlety of Sri Bhagavan's guidance — or rather of the human manipulation of his guidance, for the guidance itself is invisible. All are open books to him. He casts a penetrating glance at this disciple or that to see how his meditation is progressing; occasionally his eyes rest full upon one of them, transmitting the direct force of his Grace. And yet all this is kept as inconspicuous as possible: a glance may even be sidelong to avoid attention, a more steadfast look may be in the interval of reading a newspaper or when the recipient himself is sitting with closed eyes and unaware; this may be to guard against the twofold danger of jealousy in other devotees and conceit in the one favoured with his look.

Special attention is often shown to a newcomer — to that the devotees have grown accustomed. Perhaps a smile will greet him every time he enters the hall, he will be watched in meditation, encouraged with friendly remarks. This may continue for a few days or weeks or months, until the meditation has been kindled in his heart or until he is bound by love to Sri Bhagavan. But such is human nature that the ego also has probably fed on the attention and he has begun to ascribe it to a superiority over the other devotees that he and Sri Bhagavan alone perceive. And then he will be ignored for a while until a deeper understanding evokes a deeper response. Unfortunately, this does not always happen; sometimes the pride in a fancied pre-eminence with Sri Bhagavan remains.

At about eight-thirty the newspapers are brought in to Sri Bhagavan and unless any questions are being asked he will open some and look through them, perhaps remarking on any item of interest — though never in a way that could be taken as a political opinion. Some of the papers are sent to the Ashram itself; some are ordered privately by one devotee or another and passed on to Sri Bhagavan first, just for the pleasure of reading a paper he has touched. One can see when it is a privately-owned paper because he will slip it carefully and deftly out of its wrapper and back again after reading, so that the owner shall receive it in the same condition that it arrived.

From about ten minutes to ten till about ten past Sri Bhagavan used to walk on the Hill, but during these last few years his body is too infirm and he just walks across the Ashram ground. All rise as he leaves the hall, unless any is deep in meditation. During this recess they gather and talk in little clusters — men and women together, for it is only while sitting in the hall that they are separate. Some read their newspapers; others get their mail from Raja Iyer, the keen, serviceable little postmaster who knows everything about everybody.

Sri Bhagavan re-enters, and if those who are sitting in the hall make to rise he motions them to remain sitting. "If you get up when I enter you will have to get up for every person who enters." Once, during the hot months, an electric fan was put on the window sill beside him. He ordered the attendant to switch it off, and when the latter persisted he himself reached up and pulled out the plug. The devotees were just as hot; why should he alone have a fan? Later, ceiling fans were installed and all benefited alike.

The mail is now brought to Sri Bhagavan. A letter addressed simply 'The Maharshi, India'. A packet of flower seeds from a devotee in America to sow in the Ashram garden. Letters from devotees all over the world. Sri Bhagavan reads through each one carefully, even scrutinising the address and postmark. If it is news from any devotee who has friends in the hall he will tell them it. He himself does not answer letters. This expresses the standpoint of the *Jnani* (Enlightened One), not having relationships, not having a name to sign. Answers are written in the Ashram office and submitted to him in the afternoon when he will point out if there is anything inappropriate in them. If anything particular or personal is needed in the answer he may indicate it, but on the whole his teaching is so plain that a devotee easily learns to reiterate it verbally— it is the Grace behind the words that he alone can give.

After the letters are disposed of it may be that all sit silent, but there is no tension in the silence; it is vibrant with peace. Perhaps someone comes to take leave, some lady with tears in her eyes at having to go, and the luminous eyes of Bhagavan infuse love and strength. How can one describe those eyes? Looking into them one feels that all the world's misery, all the struggle of one's past, all the problems of the mind, fall away like a miasma from which one has been lifted into the calm reality of peace. There is no need for words; his Grace stirs one's heart and thus the outer Guru turns one inwards to awareness of the Guru within.

At eleven o'clock the Ashram gong sounds for lunch. All stand up until Sri Bhagavan has left the hall. If it is an ordinary day the devotees disperse to their homes, but perhaps it is some festival or a *bhiksha* given by one of the devotees as an offering or thanksgiving and all are invited to lunch. The large dining hall is completely bare of furniture. Pieces of banana leaf are spread out as plates in double rows breadthwise across the red-tiled floor and the devotees sit cross-legged before them. A partition in the middle stretches three-quarters of the width of the hall. At one side of it sit those Brahmins who prefer to retain their orthodoxy, at the other side non-Brahmins, non-Hindus and those Brahmins who prefer to eat with the other devotees. Provision is thus made for the orthodox, but Sri Bhagavan says nothing to induce Brahmins either to retain or discard their orthodoxy, at any rate not publicly or to all alike. He himself sits against the east wall in sight of both sections of the devotees.

Attendants and Brahmin women walk down the rows serving rice, vegetables and condiments on the leaves. All wait for Sri Bhagavan to start eating and he waits until everyone has been served. Eating is a full-time occupation, not mixed with chatter, as in the West. An American lady who finds it hard to conform to Indian customs has brought a spoon with her. One of the servers piles some vegetables on her leaf and tells her that they have been specially prepared without the hot spices used in the general cooking — Sri Bhagavan himself gave instructions for it. The rest all eat busily with their hands. Attendants pass up and down the rows, serving second helpings, water, buttermilk, fruit or sweet. Sri Bhagavan calls an attendant back to him angrily. When there is remissness in the outer technique of life he can show anger. The attendant is putting a quarter mango on every leaf and has slipped a half mango on to his. He puts it back and picks out the smallest piece he can see.

One by one the diners finish, and as each one finishes he rises and leaves, stopping to wash his hands at the tap outside before he goes home.

Until two o'clock Sri Bhagavan rests and the hall is closed to devotees. The Ashram management decided that his failing health made this midday rest necessary, but how were they to bring it about? If asked to accept an indulgence that would inconvenience the devotees he would most probably refuse. Rather than risk this they decided to make the change unofficially by privately requesting devotees not to enter the hall at that time. For a few days all went well and then a newcomer, not knowing the rule, went in after lunch. An attendant beckoned to him to come out, but Sri Bhagavan called him back to ask what it was all about. After lunch next day Sri Bhagavan was seen sitting on the steps outside the hall and when the attendant asked him what was the matter he said, "It seems that no one is allowed into the hall until two o'clock." It was only with great difficulty that he was prevailed upon to accept the hours of rest.

In the afternoon there may be new faces in the hall, for few of the devotees sit the whole day there. Even those who live near the Ashram usually have household or other tasks to see to and many have their fixed hours of attendance.

Sri Bhagavan never speaks about doctrine except in answer to a question, or only very rarely. And when he is answering questions it is not in a tone of pontifical gravity but in a conversational manner, often with wit and laughter. Nor is the questioner expected to accept anything because he says it; he is free to dispute until convinced. A Theosophist asks whether Sri Bhagavan approves of the search for invisible Masters and he retorts with swift wit, "If they are invisible how can you see them?" "In consciousness," the Theosophist replies, and then comes the real answer, "In consciousness there are no others."

Someone from another ashram asks, "Am I right in saying that the difference is that you don't ascribe reality to the world and we do?"

And Sri Bhagavan uses humour to avert discussion. "On the contrary, since we say that Being is One we ascribe full reality to the world, and what is more we ascribe full reality to God: but by saying there are three you only give one-third reality to the world, and you only give one-third reality to God."

Everyone joins in the laughter, but in spite of this some of the devotees drift into a discussion with the visitor, and then Sri Bhagavan remarks, "There is not much benefit in such discussions."

If questions are put in English he replies through an interpreter. Though he does not speak English fluently he understands everything and pulls up the interpreter if there is the slightest inaccuracy.

Although doctrinally uniform, the replies of Sri Bhagavan were very much *ad hominem*, varying considerably with the questioner. A Christian missionary asked, "Is God personal?" and, without compromising with the doctrine of Advaita, Sri Bhagavan tried to make the answer easy for him: "Yes, He is always the First Person, the 'I' ever standing before you. If you give precedence to worldly things God seems to have receded into the background; if you give up all else and seek Him alone He alone will remain as the I, the Self."

One wonders whether the missionary recalled that this is the name God proclaimed through Moses. Sri Bhagavan sometimes remarked on the excellence of 'I Am' as a Divine Name.

It is usually newcomers who ask questions and receive explanations. The disciples seldom have questions to ask, some of them never. The explanations are not the teaching; they are only a signpost to the teaching.

A quarter to five. Sri Bhagavan rubs his stiff knees and legs and reaches out for the staff. Sometimes it requires two or three efforts to rise from the couch, but he will not accept help. During the twenty minutes of his absence the hall is again swept out and the covers arranged on the couch.

Some ten or fifteen minutes after his return the chanting of the Vedas begins, followed by the *Upadesa Saram*, the 'Instruction in Thirty Verses' of Sri Bhagavan. This is one point in which Sri Bhagavan has discarded orthodoxy, for strictly speaking only Brahmins are allowed to listen to the chanting of the Vedas, whereas here all do alike. When asked what the benefit of it is he has replied simply, "The sound of the chanting helps to still the mind." He has also said explicitly that it is not necessary to learn the meaning. This is a practical illustration of what has been said about the 'meditation' he enjoined —that it is not thought but turning the mind inwards to the awareness beyond thought.

The chanting lasts about thirty-five minutes. While it is going on it often happens that he sits still, his face eternal, motionless, majestic, as though carved in rock. When it is finished all sit till six-thirty when the ladies are expected to leave the Ashram. Some of the men remain for another hour, usually in silence, sometimes talking, singing Tamil songs; and then there is supper and the devotees disperse.

The evening session is particularly precious because it combines the solemnity of the early morning chanting with the friendliness of the later hours. And yet, for those who apprehend it, the solemnity is always there, even when Sri Bhagavan is outwardly laughing and joking.

An attendant comes to massage his legs with some liniment, but he takes it away from him. They fuss over him too much. But he turns the refusal into a joke: "You have had Grace by look and by speech and now you want Grace by touch? Let me have some of the Grace by touch myself."

However, it is only a pale reflection of his humour that can be set down on paper, for it was less the things said, keen and witty though they were, than the saying of them. When he told a story he was a complete actor, reproducing the part as though he lived it. It was fascinating to watch him, even for those who did not understand the language. Real life also was a part he played and in real life the transitions could be just as swift, from humour to a deep sympathy.

Even in the early days, when he was thought to be oblivious to everything, he had a keen sense of humour, and there were jokes that he only told years later. On one occasion when his mother and a crowd of others visited him at Pavalakunru they bolted the door on the outside when they went into town for food, fearing that he might slip away. He, however, knew that the door could be lifted off its hinges and opened while still bolted, so in order to avoid the crowd and the disturbance he slipped out that way while they were gone. On their return they found the door shut and bolted but the room empty. Later, when no one was about, he returned the same way. They sat telling one another in front of him how he had disappeared through a closed door and then appeared again by means of *siddhi* (supernatural powers), and no tremor showed on his face, though years later the whole hall were shaking with laughter when he told them the story.

A word should be said also about the great annual festivals. Most of the devotees were unable to live permanently at

Tiruvannamalai and could only come occasionally, so that there were always crowds for the public holidays, especially for the four great festivals of Kartikai, Deepavali, *Mahapuja* (the anniversary of the Mother's death) and *Jayanthi* (the birthday of Sri Bhagavan). *Jayanthi* was the greatest and most heavily attended of these. At first Sri Bhagavan was reluctant to have it celebrated at all. He composed the stanzas:

> You who wish to celebrate the birthday, seek first whence was your birth. One's true birthday is when he enters That which transcends birth and death — the Eternal Being.
>
> At least on one's birthday one should mourn one's entry into this world (*samsara*). To glory in it and celebrate it is like delighting in and decorating a corpse. To seek one's Self and merge in the Self: that is wisdom.

However, for the devotees, the birth of Sri Bhagavan was cause for rejoicing and he was induced to submit; but he refused either then or on any occasion to allow puja (ritualistic worship) to be made to him. The crowd was vast and all the devotees took their meals with Sri Bhagavan that day. Even the large dining hall was inadequate; a palm leaf roofing was erected on bamboo supports over the square of ground outside and all sat there. There was also feeding of the poor, sometimes two or three relays coming to be fed, with police and boy scouts guarding the entrances and managing the crowds.

On any such day Sri Bhagavan would sit aloof, regal, and yet with an intimate look of recognition for each old devotee who came. At one of the Kartikai festivals, when the crowds packed the whole Ashram ground and a railing had been erected round him to keep them off, a little boy scrambled through the bars and ran up to him to show him his new toy. He turned to the attendant, laughing, "See how much use your railing is!"

In September 1946 a great celebration was held for the fiftieth anniversary of Sri Bhagavan's arrival at Tiruvannamalai. Devotees gathered from far and wide. A *Golden Jubilee Souvenir* was compiled of articles and poems written for the occasion.

During the last years the old hall was becoming too small even on ordinary days, and it became more usual to sit outside under a palm leaf roofing. In 1939 work had started on a temple over the Mother's samadhi, and this was completed in 1949, together with a new hall for Sri Bhagavan and the devotees to sit in. They were two parts of one building, constructed by traditional temple builders according to the *sastraic* (scriptural) rules.

The building stretches south of the old hall and the office, between them and the road. The western half of it, south of the old hall, is the temple, the eastern half is a large, square, well-ventilated hall where Sri Bhagavan was to sit with his devotees.

The *kumbhabhishekam*, or ritualistic opening of the temple and hall, was an imposing ceremony that many of the devotees attended. It crowned years of effort, work and planning. Sri Bhagavan, however, was reluctant to enter the new hall. He preferred simplicity and did not like any grandeur on his account. Many of the devotees also were reluctant — the old hall was so vibrant with his Presence and the new seemed cold and lifeless in comparison. When he entered it the last sickness had already gripped his body.

14
UPADESA

IT IS SURPRISING how secret was the *upadesa* of Sri
Bhagavan, that is to say the guidance or instruction he
gave to his disciples — there is no exact English translation
of the word. Although he was accessible to all alike, although
questions were normally asked and answered in public, the
guidance given to each disciple was nevertheless intensely
direct and adapted to his character. When asked once by
Swami Yogananda, a Swami with a large following in America,
what spiritual instruction should be given to the people for
their uplift, he replied: "It depends on the temperament and
spiritual maturity of the individual. There can be no mass
instruction." It is enough to recall the stories of four devotees
already referred to — Echammal, the Mother, Sivaprakasam

Pillai and Natesa Mudaliar — to realize how enormously the treatment varied.

Sri Bhagavan was intensely active — he himself has said so, though none who experienced his Grace needed any confirmation — and yet so concealed was his activity that casual visitors and those who failed to perceive believed that he gave no *upadesa* at all or that he was indifferent to the needs of seekers. There were many such, like the Brahmin who tried to dissuade Natesa Mudaliar from visiting him.

The extreme importance of this question lies in the fact that (except in the rarest of cases, such as that of Sri Bhagavan himself) Realization is possible only through the Grace of a Guru. Sri Bhagavan was as definite about this as other Masters. Therefore it was not enough for the *sadhaka* (aspirant) to know that his teaching was sublime and his presence inspiring; it was necessary to know that he was a Guru giving *diksha* (initiation) and *upadesa* (instruction).

The term 'Guru' is used in three senses. It can mean one who, although he has no spiritual attainment, has been invested (like the ordination of a priest) with the right to give initiation and *upadesa*. He is often hereditary and is not unlike a family doctor for spiritual health. Secondly, the Guru can be one who, in addition to the above, has some spiritual attainment and can guide his disciples by more potent *upadesa* (even though the actual practices enjoined may be the same) as far as he himself has gone. But in the highest and truest meaning of the word, the Guru is he who has realized Oneness with the Spirit that is the Self of all. This is the Sadguru.

It is in this last sense that Sri Bhagavan used the word. Therefore he said, "God, Guru and Self are the same." And in describing the Guru he said (in *Spiritual Instruction*):

"The Guru is one who at all times abides in the profound depth of the Self. He never sees any difference between himself and others and he is completely free from false notions of distinction — that he himself is the Enlightened or the Liberated while others around him are in bondage or the darkness of ignorance. His firmness or self-possession can never be shaken under any circumstances and he is never perturbed."

Submission to this Guru is not submission to any outside oneself but to the Self manifested outwardly in order to help one discover the Self within. "The Master is within; meditation is meant to remove the ignorant idea that he is only outside. If he were a stranger whom you were awaiting he would be bound to disappear also. What would be the use of a transient being like that? But as long as you think that you are separate or are the body, so long is the outer Master also necessary and he will appear as if with a body. When the wrong identification of oneself with the body ceases the Master is found to be none other than the Self."

It is axiomatic that one who is a Guru in this supreme sense of having realized his identity with the Absolute does not say so, inasmuch as there is no ego left to affirm the identity. Also he does not say that he has disciples, for, being beyond otherness, there can be no relationship for him.

Although the *Jnani* (Enlightened) is One with the Absolute, his traits of character continue to exist outwardly as the vehicle of his manifestation, so that one *Jnani* can have quite different human characteristics from another. One characteristic of Sri Bhagavan was his shrewdness and perspicacity. There seems no doubt that, just as he allowed himself to be considered a *mouni* (one who has taken a vow of silence) during his early years at Tiruvannamalai in order to avoid disturbance, so he took advantage of this doctrinal impossibility of asserting identity or admitting relationship in order to ward off unwarranted demands for *upadesa* from those who were not his real devotees. It is remarkable how successful the defence was, while real devotees were not taken in by it and were not intended to be.

Let us examine Sri Bhagavan's statements carefully. He sometimes said he had no disciples and never stated explicitly that he was the Guru; however, he used the expression 'the Guru' as equivalent to 'the *Jnani*' and in such a way as to leave no doubt that he was the Guru, and he more than once joined in singing the song 'Ramana Sadguru'.

Moreover, when a devotee was genuinely distressed and seeking a solution he would sometimes reassure him in a way that left no room for doubt. An English disciple, Major Chadwick, kept a record of such an assurance given to him in the year 1940:

C: Bhagavan says he has no disciples?

B: Yes.

C: He also says that a Guru is necessary if one wishes to attain Liberation?

B: Yes.

C: What then must I do? Has my sitting here all these years been just a waste of time? Must I go and look for some Guru in order to receive initiation seeing that Bhagavan says he is not a Guru?

B: What do you think brought you here such a long distance and made you remain so long? Why do you doubt? If there had been any need to seek a Guru elsewhere you would have gone away long ago.

The Guru or *Jnani* (Enlightened One) sees no difference between himself and others. For him all are *Jnanis*, all are one with himself, so how can a *Jnani* say that such and such is his disciple? But the unliberated one sees all as multiple, he sees all as different from himself, so to him the Guru-disciple relationship is a reality, and he needs the Grace of the Guru to waken him to reality. For him there are three ways of initiation, by touch, look and silence. (Sri Bhagavan here gave me to understand that his way was by silence, as he has to many on other occasions).

C: Then Bhagavan *does* have disciples!

B: As I said, from Bhagavan's point of view there are no disciples; but from that of the disciple the Grace of the Guru is like an ocean. If he comes with a cup he will only get a cupful. It is no use complaining of the niggardliness of the ocean; the bigger the vessel the more he will be able to carry. It is entirely up to him.

C: Then to know whether Bhagavan is my Guru or not is just a matter of faith, if Bhagavan will not admit it.

B: (Sitting straight up, turning to the interpreter and speaking with great emphasis). Ask him, does he want me to give him a written document?

Few were so persistent as Major Chadwick in their demand for an assurance. The statement involving recognition of duality would not be made, but short of that Sri Bhagavan admitted being the Guru clearly enough for any person of understanding and goodwill; and some knew it without verbal confirmation.

A. Bose, a Bengali industrialist, as recorded by S.S. Cohen, once tried to elicit a precise statement. He said, "I am convinced that a Guru is necessary for the success of the *sadhaka's* (aspirant's) efforts." Then he added, with a quizzical smile, "Does Bhagavan feel for us?"

But Sri Bhagavan turned the tables on him, "Practice is necessary for you; the Grace is always there." After a short silence he added, "You are neck deep in water and yet you cry out that you are thirsty."

Even the practice really meant making oneself receptive to the Grace; Sri Bhagavan sometimes illustrated this by saying that although the sun is shining you must make the effort of turning to look at it if you want to see it. Professor Venkatramiah records in his diary that he said to Mrs. Piggott, an English visitor, "Realization is the result of the Guru's Grace more than of teachings, lectures, meditations, etc. These are only secondary but that is the primary and essential cause."

Some who knew his teaching at second-hand suggested that he did not hold it necessary to have a Guru and explained the lack of explicit initiation in that way, but he rejected this suggestion unequivocally. S.S. Cohen has recorded a conversation on this subject with Dilip Kumar Roy, the celebrated musician of Sri Aurobindashram:

DKR: Some people report Maharshi to deny the need of a Guru.
      Others say the reverse. What does Maharshi say?
B: I have never said that there is no need for a Guru.
DKR: Sri Aurobindo often refers to you as having had no Guru.
B: That depends on what you call Guru. He need not necessarily
      be in human form. Dattatreya had twenty-four Gurus —
      the elements, etc. That means that any form in the world
      was his Guru. Guru is absolutely necessary. The
      Upanishads say that none but a Guru can take a man out

of the jungle of mental and sense perceptions, so there
must be a Guru.

DKR: I mean a human Guru. The Maharshi didn't have one.

B: I might have had at some time or other. And didn't I sing
hymns to Arunachala? What is a Guru? Guru is God or
the Self. First a man prays to God to fulfil his desires,
then a time comes when he does not pray for the fulfilment
of a desire but for God himself. So God appears to him in
some form or other, human or non-human, to guide him
as a Guru in answer to his prayer.

It was only when some visitor brought up the objection
that Sri Bhagavan himself had not had a Guru that he explained
that the Guru need not necessarily take human form, and it was
understood that this referred to very rare cases.

Perhaps it was with V. Venkatraman that he came nearest
to an explicit admission that he was the Guru. He told him
once: "Two things are to be done, first to find the Guru outside
yourself and then to find the Guru within. You have already
done the first."

Or perhaps the confirmation that I myself received was
even more explicit. After some weeks at the Ashram I perceived
that Sri Bhagavan really was a Guru giving initiation and
guidance. I wrote to inform friends in Europe of this and, before
sending the letter, I showed it to Sri Bhagavan and asked whether
to send it. He approved of it and, handing it back, said, "Yes,
send it."

To be a Guru is to give initiation and *upadesa*. The two are
inseparable, for there is no *upadesa* without the initial act of
initiation and no point in initiation unless it is to be followed
up with *upadesa*. The question, therefore, sometimes took the
form of whether Sri Bhagavan gave initiation or *upadesa*.

When asked whether he gave initiation Sri Bhagavan always avoided a direct answer. Had the answer been 'no' he would most certainly have said 'no'; but had he said 'yes' the defence against unwarranted demands for initiation would have been down and it would have become necessary to accept some and reject others by a decision that would have appeared arbitrary instead of letting their own understanding or lack of understanding make the decision. His most usual form of reply was that given to Major Chadwick, "There are three modes of initiation, by touch, by look and by silence." This was the practice usual to Sri Bhagavan of making an impersonal doctrinal utterance in which, however, the answer to the specific question was to be found. The statement is well known, the three modes of initiation — according to the Hindus — being typified by the bird, which needs to sit on its eggs in order to hatch them, the fish, which needs only to look at them, and the tortoise, which needs only to think of them. Initiation by look or by silence has become very rare in this age; it is the *mouna diksha* of Arunachala, of Dakshinamurti, and is the mode of initiation particularly appropriate to the direct path of Self-enquiry which Sri Bhagavan taught. It was, therefore, doubly suitable, both inherently and as affording a convenient camouflage.

The initiation by look was a very real thing. Sri Bhagavan would turn to the devotee, his eyes fixed upon him with blazing intentness. The luminosity, the power of his eyes pierced into one, breaking down the thought-process. Sometimes it was as though an electric current was passing through one, sometimes a vast peace, a flood of light. One devotee has described it: "Suddenly Bhagavan turned his luminous, transparent eyes on me. Before that I could not stand his gaze for long. Now I looked straight back into those powerful and wonderful eyes, how long I could not tell. They held me in a sort of vibration distinctly audible to me." Always it was followed by the feeling, the indubitable conviction, that one had been taken up by Sri Bhagavan, that henceforth he was in charge, he was guiding. Those who knew would perceive when such an initiation took place, but it would usually be inconspicuous; it might happen during the chanting of the Vedas, when few would be watching or the devotee might feel a sudden impulse to go to Sri Bhagavan before daybreak or at some time when few or none would be present. The initiation by silence was equally real. It entered into those who turned to Sri Bhagavan in their hearts without being able to go bodily to Tiruvannamalai. Sometimes it was given in a dream, as with Natesa Mudaliar.

No Master was more categorical than Sri Bhagavan about his guidance and protection once a devotee had been taken up and the silent initiation given. He assured Sivaprakasam Pillai in the exposition that was later published as *Who am I?*: "He that has won the Grace of the Guru shall undoubtedly be saved and never forsaken, just as the prey that has fallen into the tiger's jaws will never be allowed to escape."

A Dutch devotee, L. Hartz, being able to stay only a short time, and perhaps fearing that his determination might weaken when he left, asked for an assurance and was told, "Even if you let go of Bhagavan, Bhagavan will never let go of you."

Two other devotees, a Czech diplomat and a Muslim professor, struck by the unusual force and directness of the assurance, asked whether it applied only to Hartz or to all the devotees and were told, "To all."

On another occasion, a devotee grew despondent at seeing no progress in himself and said, "I am afraid if I continue like this I shall go to hell." And Sri Bhagavan replied, "If you do Bhagavan will go after you and bring you back."

Even the circumstances of the devotee's life are shaped by the Guru so as to promote his *sadhana* (spiritual progress). One devotee was told, "The Master is both within and without, so he creates conditions to drive you inwards and at the same time prepares the interior to drag you to the Centre."

If one who was not turned to Sri Bhagavan in his heart asked whether he gave *upadesa* he might make some enigmatic reply or none at all, and in either case a negative answer would be presumed. In fact, his *upadesa*, like his initiation, was through silence. The mind was silently turned in the direction in which it should strive. A devotee was expected to understand this. Very few needed verbal assurance.

The story of V. Venkatraman, who has already been referred to, is illustrative. In his youth he was a great devotee of Sri Ramakrishna, but he felt the need for a living Guru in flesh and blood, so he prayed to him with the fervour of intense longing, "Master, grant me a living Guru no less perfect than yourself." Very soon afterwards he heard of Sri Ramana, then but a few years in the Ashram at the foot of the Hill. He went there with an offering of flowers. It so happened (as would always happen when desirable) that there was no one else in the hall when he arrived. Sri Bhagavan was reclining on the couch, behind him on the wall the portrait of Sri Ramakrishna to which Venkatraman had prayed. Sri Bhagavan cut the garland in half; one half he bade the attendant place upon his portrait and the other on the temple lingam. Venkatraman had a feeling of lightness and ease. He was at home, his purpose achieved. He told the story of his coming. Sri Bhagavan asked him, "You know about Dakshinamurti?"

"I know that he gave silent *upadesa*," he replied.

And Sri Bhagavan said, "That is the *upadesa* you will get here."

This silent *upadesa* was in fact very varied. Sri Bhagavan spoke and wrote most about the *vichara* or Self-enquiry, and therefore the opinion arose that he prescribed only *Jnana-marga*, the Path of Knowledge, which most people find too sheer in this age. But in fact he was universal and provided guidance for every temperament, by the path of Devotion no less than of Knowledge. Love and devotion to him are a bridge across the abyss to salvation. He had many devotees for whom he prescribed no other path.

The same Venkatraman grew uneasy after some time at being given no *sadhana* — that is no practice to perform — and complained.

"And what brought you here?" Sri Bhagavan asked.

"Thinking of you, Swami."

"Then that is also your *sadhana*. That is sufficient." And indeed, the thought or remembrance of Bhagavan began to accompany him everywhere, to become inseparable from him.

The path of devotion is the same really as that of submission. The whole burden is cast upon the Guru. This also Sri Bhagavan enjoined. To one devotee he said, "Submit to me and I will strike down the mind." To another he said, "Only keep quiet, Bhagavan will do the rest." He told another, Devaraja Mudaliar, "Your business is only to surrender and leave everything to me." And he often said, "There are two ways: either ask yourself 'Who am I?' or surrender to the Guru."

And yet, to surrender, to keep the mind still and be fully receptive to the Grace of the Guru, is not easy. It requires constant effort, constant remembering, and only the Grace of the Guru makes it possible. Many used devotional or other practices to help them in the attempt, and Sri Bhagavan approved and authorised such means, though he seldom actually prescribed them.

Most potent, though invisible, was the power of *sat sangh*. Literally this means 'association with Being', but as a means of *sadhana* it is used to mean 'association with one who has realized Sat or Being'. Sri Bhagavan spoke of it in the highest terms. The first five of the *Supplementary Forty Verses* are devoted to its praise. The story of their inclusion is characteristic. The adopted daughter of Echammal found one of them written in Sanskrit on the paper in which a packet of sweets was wrapped and was so moved by it that she learned it and recited it before Sri Bhagavan, and he, seeing its importance, translated it into Tamil. At the time when he was compiling the forty supplementary verses, writing some and translating others, and this verse with the four others, also from Sanskrit, were included. The third of them gives association with a Master pre-eminence over all other methods. "If association with Sages is obtained to what purpose are the various methods of self-discipline? Tell me, of what use is a fan when the cool, gentle, southern breeze is blowing?"

Association with Sri Bhagavan worked a subtle alchemy, even though its effects might only become visible years later. He sometimes told devotees explicitly of its value to them. To Ranga Aiyar, the school friend referred to in Chapter Three, he once said, "If you stay with the *Jnani* he gives you your cloth ready woven," the implication being that by other methods you are given the thread and have to weave it yourself.

Sundaresa Aiyar became a devotee at the age of twelve. When he got to be about nineteen he grew dissatisfied with himself, feeling that more conscious and intense effort was needed. He was a householder, living in town, but had been visiting Sri Bhagavan almost daily; now, however, he decided, as an act of stern discipline, not to go again until he had developed such detachment and earnestness of purpose as to make him worthy of the association. For a hundred days he stayed away, and then the thought came to him, "How am I better for not seeing Bhagavan?" And he went. Sri Bhagavan met him at the entrance to Skandashram and greeted him with the question, "How are you better for not visiting me?" He then spoke to him of the importance and potency of *sat sangh* even though the disciple did not perceive the effect it was having on him or see any improvement in himself. He compared it to a mother feeding her child during its sleep at night, so that next day the child thinks it took no food, although she knows it did and in fact the food sustains it.

This example implies more than an automatic benefit from living within the atmosphere of a Sage; it implies conscious direction of the influence by him. On one occasion Sri Bhagavan gave striking confirmation of this, though those who had experienced it needed none. Sundaresa Aiyar composed a Tamil song in his praise referring to the Grace flowing forth from his eyes to sustain the devotees, and Sri Bhagavan corrected him, "No, not flowing but projected, because it is a conscious process directing the Grace to the persons chosen."

The disciple also has to make effort in order to utilise fully the Grace of the Master, and for this the method that Sri Bhagavan constantly propounded was the *vichara*, the question 'Who am I?' This was the *sadhana* he brought to meet the needs of our age and about this there was no secrecy or concealment. He was quite categorical about its pre-eminence. "Self-enquiry is the one infallible means, the only direct one, to realize the unconditioned, absolute Being that you really are.... The attempt to destroy the ego or mind through *sadhanas* other than Self-enquiry is like the thief turning policeman to catch the thief that is himself. Self-enquiry alone can reveal the truth that neither the ego nor the mind really exists and enable one to realize the pure, undifferentiated Being of the Self or Absolute. Having realized the Self, nothing remains to be known, because it is perfect Bliss, it is the All." (*Maharshi's Gospel*, Part II.)

"The purpose of Self-enquiry is to focus the entire mind at its Source. It is not, therefore, a case of one 'I' searching for another 'I'." (*ibid.*)

To focus the entire mind at its Source is to turn it inward upon itself. The instruction was to sit in meditation, asking 'Who am I?' at the same time focussing the attention on the heart, not the physical organ on the left side of the chest but the spiritual heart on the right. According to the nature of the questioner, Sri Bhagavan would lay stress first on the physical or the mental aspect, the concentration on the Heart or the question 'Who am I?'

The spiritual heart on the right site of the chest is not one of the yogic *chakras* (centres); it is the centre and source of the ego-self and the abode of the Self and is therefore the place of Union. When asked whether there was any scriptural or other authority for locating the Heart at this spot, Sri Bhagavan said that he had found that it is so and had later seen it confirmed in one Malayalam book on ayurveda.[1] (an Indian system of medicine.) Those who have followed his injunctions have also found it so. This is so fundamental to the use of the *vichara* that it will be worthwhile reproducing here a conversation from *Maharshi's Gospel* in which Sri Bhagavan explained it at some length.

---

[1] *Cf.* "The wise man's heart is at his right hand but a fool's heart is at his left". *Ecclestiastes*, x, 2.

Devotee: Sri Bhagavan has specified a particular place for the Heart within the physical body, that is in the chest, two digits to the right from the median.

Bhagavan: Yes, that is the Centre of spiritual experience according to the testimony of the Sages. This Spiritual Heart-centre is quite different from the blood-propelling, muscular organ known by the same name. The spiritual Heart-centre is not an organ of the body. All that you can say of the Heart is that it is the very Core of your being, that with which you are really identical (as the word in Sanskrit literally means) whether you are awake, asleep or dreaming, whether you are engaged in work or immersed in *samadhi*.

D: In that case, how can it be localised in any part of the body? Fixing a place for the Heart would imply setting physiological limitations to That which is beyond space and time.

B: That is true, but the person who puts the question about the position of the Heart regards himself as existing with or in the body. . . . Since, during the bodiless experience of the Heart as pure Consciousness, the Sage is not at all aware of the body, that absolute experience is localised by him within the limits of the physical body by a sort of recollection made while he is with bodily awareness.

D: For men like me who have neither the direct experience of the Heart nor the consequent recollection, the matter seems to be somewhat difficult to grasp. About the position of the Heart itself, perhaps, we must depend on some sort of guesswork.

B: If the determination of the position of the Heart depended on guesswork, even for the ignorant, the question would be scarcely worth consideration. No, it is not on guesswork that you have to depend but on an unerring intuition.

D: Who has this intuition?

B: Everybody.

D: Does Sri Bhagavan credit me with an intuitive knowledge of the Heart?

B: No, not of the Heart but of the position of the Heart in relation to your identity.

D: Did Sri Bhagavan say that I intuitively know the position of the Heart in the physical body?

B: Why not?

D: (pointing to himself) Is it to me personally that Sri Bhagavan is referring?

B: Yes. That is the intuition. How did you refer to yourself by gesture just now? Did you not point your finger to the right side of your chest? That is exactly the place of the Heart-Centre.

D: So then, in the absence of direct knowledge of the Heart-Centre, I have to depend on this intuition?

B: What is wrong with it? When a schoolboy says, "It is I that did the sum right", or when he asks you, "Shall I run and get the book for you?" does he point to the head that did the sum right or to the legs that will carry him quickly to get the book? No, in both cases his finger is pointed quite naturally towards the right side of the chest, thus giving innocent expression to the profound truth that the Source of I-ness in him is there. It is an unerring intuition that makes him refer to himself, to the Heart that is the Self, in that way. The act is quite involuntary and universal, that is to say it is the same in the case of every individual. What stronger proof than this do you require about the position of the Heart-centre in the physical body?

The instruction, then, was to sit concentrating on the heart at the right side and ask 'Who am I?' When thoughts arise during the meditation one is not to follow them up but to watch them and ask: 'What is this thought? Where did it come from? And to whom? To me — and who am I?' So each thought disappears when scrutinised and is turned back to the basic I-thought. If impure thoughts rise up they are to be treated in the same way, for *sadhana* really does what psycho-analysis claims to do — it clears out the filth from the subconscious, brings it up to the light of day and destroys it. "Yes, all kinds of thoughts arise in meditation. That is only right, for what lies hidden in you is brought out. Unless it rises up how can it be destroyed?" (*Maharshi's Gospel.*)

All thought-forms are alien to this mode of meditation. Sometimes a devotee would ask Sri Bhagavan if he could use a theme such as 'I am He', or any other, during the enquiry but he always forbade it. On one occasion when a devotee had suggested one theme after another, he explained: "All thoughts are inconsistent with Realization. The right thing to do is to exclude thoughts of oneself and all other thoughts. Thought is one thing and Realization is quite another."

There is no answer to the Who-am-I question. There can be no answer, for it is dissolving the I-thought, which is the parent of all other thoughts, and piercing beyond to the stillness where thought is not. "Suggestive replies to the enquiry, such as *Sivoham* (I am Siva) are not to be given to the mind during meditation. The true answer will come of itself. No answer the ego can give can be right." The answer is the awakening current of awareness mentioned at the end of Chapter One, vibrating as the very essence of one's being and yet impersonal. By constant practice this is to be made more and more frequent until it becomes continuous, not only during mediation but underlying speech and action also. Even then the *vichara* is still to be used, for the ego will try to make a truce with the current of awareness and if it is once tolerated it will gradually grow to power and then fight to recover supremacy, like the Gentiles whom the Hebrews allowed to remain in the Promised Land. Sri Bhagavan insisted (for instance, in his replies to Sivaprakasam Pillai) that the enquiry is to be kept up to the very end. Whatever states, whatever powers, whatever perceptions or visions may come, there is always the question of to whom they come until the Self alone remains.

Indeed, visions and powers can prove a distraction, clamping the mind down as effectively as attachment to physical power or pleasure and deluding it into imagining that it has been metamorphosed into the Self. And, as with earthly powers and pleasures, the desire for them is even more injurious than their possession. Narasimhaswami was once sitting before Sri Bhagavan, translating into Tamil the life and sayings of Vivekananda. Coming upon the description of the well-known incident when a single touch by Sri Ramakrishna gave Vivekananda the perception of all things as one substance, the thought struck him whether such a perception was not desirable and whether Sri Bhagavan could give it to him also by touch or look. As so often happened, the question that troubled him was raised at that very moment by another devotee: Echammal asked whether *siddhis* (powers) could be attained by the devotees. It was the period when Sri Bhagavan was composing the *Forty Verses on Reality*, the work which, with its Supplement, can be taken as his enunciation of doctrine, and he composed a stanza in answer to the question. "To abide firm in the Reality which is eternal is the true *siddhi*. Other attainments are all such as are possessed in dreams. Do they prove real when one awakes? Will those who are established in Reality and free from illusion care for such things?"

The occult is an obstacle to the spiritual. Powers and, even more, the desire for powers, impede the aspirant. It is said in the *Devikalottram*, which Sri Bhagavan translated from Sanskrit into Tamil: "One should not accept thaumaturgic powers, etc., even when directly offered to one, for they are like ropes to tether a beast and will sooner or later drag one down. Supreme *Mukti* (Liberation) does not lie that way; it is not found elsewhere than in Infinite Consciousness."

To return from this digression: it is not only as a technique of meditation that Sri Bhagavan prescribed Self-enquiry but as a technique of living also. Asked whether it should be used always or just in fixed hours of meditation, he replied, "Always." This throws light upon his refusal to sanction renunciation of worldly life, for the very circumstances which had been obstacles to *sadhana* were thus converted into instruments of *sadhana*. Ultimately, *sadhana* is simply an attack on the ego, and no amount of ecstasy or meditation can carry it to success so long as the ego remains entrenched in hope and fear, ambition and resentment, in any sort of passion or desire. Sri Rama and King Janaka were free from attachment although they lived in the world; the sadhu who tried to roll down rocks on Sri Bhagavan was bound by it although he had renounced the world.

At the same time, this does not mean that mere unselfish action is sufficient without any plan of campaign, for the ego is subtle and tenacious and will take refuge even in those actions that are intended to destroy it, taking pride in humility or enjoying austerity.

Self-enquiry in daily activity, asking oneself to whom any thought occurs, is a plan of campaign and a very potent one. It may not seem so when applied to an unemotional thought, say to one's opinion of a book or a film; but applied to an emotional thought it has terrific potency and strikes at the very root of the passions. One has been hurt and feels resentment — who is hurt or resentful? Who is pleased or despondent, angry or triumphant? One falls into daydreaming or visualise possible triumphs and thus inflates the ego as powerfully as meditation deflates it; and at such a moment it requires strength and alertness to draw the sword of *vichara* and cut through the entanglement.

In the activities of life also, Sri Bhagavan enjoined surrender and submission to the Divine Will side by side with *vichara*. He compared a person who thought he was bearing his own burdens and responsibilities to a passenger in a train who insists on carrying his luggage even though the train is taking it along just the same and a wiser passenger puts it on the rack and sits back comfortably. All the injunctions and examples he gave converge on the one point of weakening self-interest and assailing the I-am-the-doer illusion.

A famous Congress worker, Jamnalal Bajaj, once came to the Ashram and asked, "Is the desire, for *swaraj* (political independence) right?"

Sri Bhagavan replied: "Yes, prolonged practical work for the goal gradually widens the outlook so that the individual gradually becomes merged in the country. Such merging of the individual is desirable and the karma is *nishkamyakarma*."

Jubilant, perhaps, at having got the Swami to approve of his political aims and desiring a still more definite assurance, Jamnalal now asked what seemed to follow logically, "If *swaraj* is gained after a prolonged struggle and terrible sacrifice is not the person justified in being pleased with the result?"

But he was disappointed. "No, in the course of the struggle he should have surrendered himself to a Higher Power whose Might must be kept in mind and never lost sight of. How then can he be elated? He should not even care for the results of his actions. Only then it becomes *nishkamya*."

That is to say that the outcome of one's activity rests with God, and all that one is responsible for is the purity and disinterestedness of it. Moreover, by doing what is right simply because it is right, without self-interest, one is benefiting others even apart from the visible results achieved and in a more potent although more subtle manner than results can indicate. One is also benefiting oneself in a very direct way. In fact, disinterested activity may be said to be the true bank account, accumulating good karma which will shape one's future destiny.

In a case like this, when questioned by some visitor, Sri Bhagavan explained what attitude of mind could make social or political activity a valid *sadhana*, but he discouraged his devotees from taking up such activity. It was enough that they should perform their own functions in life with purity and disinterestedness, doing what was right because it was right. Even though the present state of the world seems inharmonious, it is part of a vaster harmony; and by developing Self-knowledge one can both know this harmony and exert a far greater harmonious influence than by attempts to change the course of events. Sri Bhagavan's teaching in this matter is summed up in a conversation with Paul Brunton:

PB: Will Maharshi give his opinion on the future of the world, as we are living in critical times?

B: Why should you worry about the future? You don't even know the present properly. Take care of the present and the future will take care of itself.

PB: Will the world soon enter a new era of friendliness and mutual help or will it go down in chaos and war?

B: There is One who governs the world and it is His task to look after the world. He who has given life to the world knows how to look after it also. He bears the burden of this world, not you.

PB: Yet if one looks around with unprejudiced eyes it is hard to see where this benevolent regard comes in.

B: As you are, so is the world. Without understanding yourself what is the use of trying to understand the world? This is a question that seekers after Truth need not consider. People waste their energies over all such questions. First find out the Truth behind yourself, then you will be in a better position to understand the Truth behind the world of which yourself is part.

It should be noted that in this last sentence Sri Bhagavan is using the word 'yourself' to mean the ego, what the questioner at the moment took to be himself. The real Self is not a part of the world but the Self and Creator of the world.

The injunction for the use of Self-enquiry in the activities of life was an extension of its traditional use and an adaptation to the needs of our time. In its direct use as meditation it is the purest and most ardent (ancient) *sadhana*. Although it came to Sri Bhagavan spontaneously and untaught, it is in the tradition of the ancient Rishis. The Sage Vasishta wrote: "This enquiry 'Who am I?' is the quest of the Self and is said to be the fire that burns up the seed of the poisonous growth of conceptual thought." However, it had formerly existed only as pure *Jnana-marga* (Path of Knowledge), simplest as well as most profound, the ultimate secret to be imparted only to those of purest understanding and to be followed by them in constant meditation, away from the distractions of the world. *Karma-marga* (the path of Action), on the other hand, had been the path for those who remained in the life of the world and consisted, as defined in the *Bhagavad Gita*, in a life of service and in acting without being attached to the fruits of one's actions, that is so say disinterestedly, with no trace of egoism. These two paths are now fused into one, making a new path suited to the new conditions of our age, a path that can be followed silently, in office or workshop no less than in ashram or cave, with or without outer observances, simply a time for meditation and then remembrance throughout the day.

"In the end all that was hidden shall be made known." Doctrinally, this saying of Christ's is fulfilled by the own proclamation of the ultimate and most secret path and by its adaptation to our age. This is what Sri Bhagavan has done.

Indeed, the new path is more than a fusion of *Jnana-marga* and *karma-marga*; it is *bhakti* (love or devotion) also, for it generates pure love — love for the Self, the Inner Guru, which is love of Bhagavan, love of God. Sri Bhagavan has said in *Maharshi's Gospel*: "The eternal, unbroken, natural state of abiding in the Self is *Jnana*. To abide in the Self you must love the Self. Since God is in fact the Self, love of the Self is love of God, and that is *bhakti*. *Jnana* and *bhakti* are thus one and the same."

The ways of *Jnana* and *bhakti* that Sri Bhagavan enjoined may seem quite different paths but actually they are far closer together than might appear, and one does not preclude the other; in fact they can fuse into the single, integral path just described.

On the one hand, submission to the outer Guru leads, through his Grace, to the inner Guru that the *vichara* seeks to discover; and, on the other hand, *vichara* leads to quietude and submission. Both methods strive after the direct subsidence of the mind, only in one case more before the outer and in the other more before the inner Guru. Indirect methods of *sadhana* seek rather to strengthen and build up the mind in order that it may eventually attain sufficient strength and amplitude to surrender before the Spirit, and it is this that Sri Bhagavan referred to as 'the thief turning policeman to catch the thief that is himself'. It is, of course, true that the mind must be strengthened and purified before it will surrender, but with the use of the *vichara* under the Grace of Sri Bhagavan this happens automatically.

A devotee, Krishna Jivrajani, once asked about this, "It is said in books that one should cultivate all the good or *daivic* (divine) qualities in order to prepare oneself for Self-realization."

And Sri Bhagavan replied: "All good or *daivic* qualities are included in *Jnana* (Knowledge) and all evil or asuric qualities in *ajnana* (ignorance). When *Jnana* comes all *ajnana* goes and all *daivic* qualities come automatically. If a man is a *Jnani* he cannot utter a lie or do anything wrong. It is, no doubt, said in some books that one should cultivate one quality after another and thus prepare for ultimate *Moksha* (Deliverance), but for those who follow the *Jnana* or *vichara marga* their *sadhana* is quite enough in itself for acquiring all *daivic* qualities; they need not do anything else."

It may, however, be asked how accessible the *vichara* is in fact. It is reported in *Spiritual Instruction*, compiled shortly after Sri Bhagavan came down from Skandashram, that a devotee asked, "Is it possible for all seekers, whatever their spiritual equipment, to adopt straight away and put into practice this method of enquiry in quest of the Self?" And that he replied: "No, it is intended only for ripe souls. Others should get the necessary training and practice by adopting such other methods as are suited to their individual development, mental and moral."

From the Virupaksha period also a similar reply is reported in the elucidations published as *Sri Ramana Gita*. The 'other methods' include religious and devotional observances, meditation, invocation, mantras, also breath-control. Not only are these preparatory to the use of the *vichara* but they may be used concurrently with it. Many devotees told Sri Bhagavan that they used such methods prescribed by some guru or asked his authorisation to use them, and he listened graciously and approved. But when any found these other methods fall away he approved of that also. A devotee told him that he no longer found any support from the other methods he had formerly used and asked his authorisation to drop them, and he replied, "Yes, all other methods only lead up to the *vichara*."

During the later period in the Ashram at the foot of the Hill, there is no record of any such limitation on the use of the *vichara* being stipulated, whereas one did hear it explicitly enjoined, together with concentration on the heart, on all who asked the way. This may lead to the conclusion that, in the new form in which Sri Bhagavan presented it, the *vichara* had only then been made really accessible to all who, through his Grace, aspired to use it.

On the other hand, it was also observed that, so far as evidence is available, few did aspire to use it. Indeed, many who came to the Ashram and asked for an elucidation of life's mystery or for some discipline to bring them peace or to purify and strengthen their character were patently so far from understanding the doctrine of Advaita or practising the *sadhana* of Self-enquiry that it was hard for the superficial observer not to feel disappointed or annoyed at the small solace they seemed to be given. But only the superficial, for as one observed more closely one perceived that the real reply was not verbal but was the silent influence that began to permeate the mind of the questioner.

In his expositions Sri Bhagavan adhered to the ultimate truth which alone the *Jnani* recognises, just as he adhered to the dictum that, being beyond otherness, the *Jnani* has no relationship and therefore calls none his disciple; but his silent Grace, acting upon the mind, enabled it to seek out for itself the most appropriate 'other methods' for its development, as has been said already in speaking of those who simply strove to surrender and keep the mind quiet. Verbal injunctions were not necessary. Each was helped according to his nature, in proportion to his understanding and devotion. "The Grace of the Guru is like an ocean. If one comes with a cup he will only get a cupful. It is no use complaining of the niggardliness of the ocean. The bigger the vessel the more one will be able to carry. It is entirely up to him."

An elderly French lady, the mother of one of the devotees, came on a visit to the Ashram. She neither understood nor cared to understand the philosophy, but from the time of her visit she became a devout Catholic although she had been little more than a nominal one before; and she recognised that the change was due to the influence of Sri Bhagavan. It was developments like this more than verbal expositions that constituted his teaching.

It may also be that, with the passage of time, the ever-increasing graciousness of Sri Bhagavan was binding the devotees to him more closely and thus preparing their hearts for the *vichara* through devotion. Not only devotees but more casual visitors also perceived how gentle, how effulgent his face became in the last years. Through Love he led up to Knowledge, just as the *vichara* leads through Knowledge to Love. Devotion to him turned the mind inwards to the Self he manifested, just as the quest of the Self within awakened unbounded love of the Self manifested in him.

One devotee expresses it: "To look at his face, so gripping, so incredibly gracious and so wise, yet with the innocence of a new-born child — he knows everything there is to know. Sometimes a vibration starts in the heart — Bhagavan — it is the core of my being taken shape, my own externalised heart — Who am I? — And thus love leads to enquiry."

It has not been normal for a Master to describe the technique of *sadhana* openly in speech and writing, as Sri Bhagavan did. This is because such technique has been effective only when imparted to the user of it as *upadesa* by his Guru. Sri Bhagavan's innovation in this matter raises from a different point of view the question how accessible is the *vichara*: how accessible can any *sadhana* be that has not been personally enjoined by the Guru?

Sri Bhagavan himself endorsed the universal tradition that the technique of *sadhana* is valid only when enjoined by the Guru. When asked once whether a man could benefit by mantras picked up anyhow, he replied, "No, he must be initiated into them."

How is it, then, that he explained the *vichara* openly and sometimes even referred visitors to the written expositions in his books? The only explanation is that he is far more than the Guru of those few who were able to approach him physically in Tiruvannamalai. His is the authority and he gave the sanction. In this spiritually dark age when many seek but a Guru is rare to find, Bhagavan Himself took form on earth as the Sadguru, the Divine Guide, of all who turn to him and proclaimed a *sadhana* accessible to all who, through his Grace, find it accessible.

Not only was the use of the *vichara* not confined to those who could go to Tiruvannamalai, it was also not confined to Hindus. The teaching of Sri Bhagavan is the essence of all religions, proclaiming openly that which was hidden. Advaita is the central postulate of Taoism and Buddhism; the doctrine of the Inner Guru is the doctrine of the 'Christ in you' restored to the plenitude of its meaning; the *vichara* penetrates to the ultimate truth of the Islamic creed or *shahada*, that there is no god but God — that there is no self but the Self. Sri Bhagavan was beyond the differences between religions. Hindu books were available to him, so he read them and expounded according to their terms, but he was also prepared to expound in the terms of other religions when asked. The *sadhana* he enjoined was not dependent on any religion. Not only Hindus came to him but Buddhists, Christians, Muslims, Jews, Parsis, and he never expected any to change his religion. Devotion to the Guru and the flow of his Grace leads to the deeper reality of every religion, and Self-enquiry to the ultimate Truth behind all religion.

15
THE DEVOTEES

ON THE WHOLE the devotees were very normal people. By no means all were scholars or intellectuals. In fact, it not infrequently happened that some intellectual preoccupied with his theories would fail to perceive the living Truth and drift away, while some simple person would remain and worship and, by his sincerity, draw on himself the Grace of Bhagavan. Because self enquiry is called *Jnana-marga*, the Path of Knowledge, it is sometimes supposed that only intellectuals can follow it, but what is meant is understanding of the heart, not theoretical knowledge. Theoretical or doctrinal knowledge may be a help but it may equally well be a hindrance.

Sri Bhagavan wrote: "What avails the learning of those who do not seek to wipe out the letters of fate by asking, 'Whence is the birth of us who know the letters?' They have made themselves like a gramophone. What else are they, Oh Arunachala? It is the unlearned who are saved rather than those whose ego has not subsided despite their learning" (*Supplementary Forty Verses*, vv. 35-36). The words about wiping out the letters of fate refer to the Hindu conception of a man's destiny being written upon his brow and mean the same, therefore, as transcending one's karma. They are a further confirmation of what was said in Chapter Five, that the doctrine of destiny does not take away the possibility of effort, or indeed the necessity for it.

Learning was not condemned in itself, just as material wealth and psychic powers were not; only, with all three alike, the desire for them and preoccupation with them were condemned as blinding a man and distracting him from the true goal. As is stated about psychic powers in an ancient text already quoted, they are like ropes to tether a beast. It was sincerity that was required, not brilliance; understanding, not theory; humility, not mental pride. Particularly when songs were sung in the hall one would see this, noticing the perfunctory interest Sri Bhagavan might show to some celebrity and the radiance of his Grace showered on one who sang with true devotion even if with little skill.

Naturally, Hindus were the most numerous among the devotees, but there were many others also. None did more to spread knowledge of Sri Bhagavan through the world than Paul Brunton with his book, *A Search in Secret India*.

Among the permanent residents in or around the Ashram in later years were Major Chadwick, large, military and benevolent, with a booming voice; Mrs. Taleyarkhan, a Parsi lady with an imperious nature and the air of a *grande dame;*

S.S. Cohen from Iraq, quiet and unobtrusive; Dr. Hafiz Syed, a retired professor of Persian, with something of the old-world charm of a Muslim aristocrat. Visitors came for longer or shorter periods from America, France, Germany, Holland, Czechoslovakia, Poland, from many lands.

Viswanathan, a younger relative of Sri Bhagavan, came in 1923 as a nineteen-year-old youth and remained. It was not his first visit, but this time as soon as he entered the hall Sri Bhagavan asked him, "Have you taken leave of your parents?"

The question was a recognition that this time he had come to stay. He admitted that, like Sri Bhagavan himself, he had simply left a note, not saying where he was going. Sri Bhagavan made him write a letter, but in any case the youth's father guessed where he had gone and came to talk it over. He had an open mind about it. He had heard glowing reports of the Swami but he had known him as a younger relative in the days when he was Venkataraman and naturally found it hard to conceive of him as Divine. Coming into the Presence, his body quivered with awe and he had fallen on his face before he knew it had happened.

"I see nothing of the old Venkataraman here!" he exclaimed.

And Sri Bhagavan laughed: "Oh, that fellow! He disappeared long ago."

Speaking to Viswanathan in his usual humorous way, Sri Bhagavan once said, "At least you knew Sanskrit when you left home; when I left home I knew nothing."

There were others also who knew Sanskrit and had studied the Scriptures, among them the retired Professor Munagala Venkatramiah (compiler of *Talks with Sri Ramana Maharshi*), who lived as a sadhu and for some years kept an Ashram diary, and the schoolmaster Sundaresa Aiyar, already referred to, who carried on his profession in Tiruvannamalai.

In the same year as Viswanathan, Muruganar also came, one of the foremost of Tamil poets. Sri Bhagavan himself would sometimes refer to his poems or have them read out. It was he who put together the *Forty Verses* and made a book of them, and he has also written an outstanding Tamil commentary on them. The musician Manavasi Ramaswami Aiyar is a still older devotee. Senior in years to Sri Bhagavan, he came to him first in 1907. He also composed beautiful songs in praise of the Master.

Ramaswami Pillai came as a youth straight from college in 1911 and stayed. Like Viswanathan and Muruganar, he remained a sadhu; however, in his case the path was rather through devotion and service. Once in 1947 Sri Bhagavan injured his foot on a stone during his daily walk on the Hill. Next day Ramaswami Pillai, grey haired already but still robust, set out to make steps and a path up the hillside. Single-handed he worked, from dawn to dusk, day after day until the path was finished, the edges firmly shored up with stone, steps chiselled out where there was a rock platform, built up where there was an earthen slope. It was well and thoroughly constructed, so thoroughly that the monsoon rains have not washed it away since; however, it has not been kept in repair because shortly after it was finished Sri Bhagavan's failing health compelled him to give up his walks on the Hill.

Ranga Aiyar, the old school friend already referred to, never settled down at Tiruvannamalai but he and his family used to come on frequent visits. He had studied in the same class as Sri Bhagavan and had played and wrestled with him, and he always enjoyed great freedom in talking and joking. Coming in the early Virupaksha days to see what his old friend looked like as a Swami, he immediately recognised that he stood before Divinity. Not so his elder brother, Mani. He stood looking scornfully at the young Swami he had known as a junior at school. Sri Bhagavan returned the look and under the impact Mani fell at his feet. After that he also became a devotee. One of Ranga Aiyar's sons wrote a long Tamil poem celebrating the 'marriage' of Sri Bhagavan with Divine Knowledge (*Jnana*).

A large part of *Maharshi's Gospel* was compiled from conversations with the Polish refugee, M. Frydman. Two Polish ladies are well-known figures at the Ashram. When Mrs. Noye had to return to her native America she could not restrain her tears. Sri Bhagavan consoled her: "Why do you weep? I am with you wherever you go."

It is true of all Bhagavan's devotees. He is always with them; if they remember him he will remember them; even if they let go of him he will not let go of them, nevertheless to have it said to one personally was a great blessing.

My three children, the only European children at Tiruvannamalai, were conspicuous among the devotees. One evening in December 1946 Sri Bhagavan initiated the two elder of them into meditation, and if their efforts to describe it fail, so do those of older people. Kitty, who was ten, wrote: "When I was sitting in the hall this evening Bhagavan smiled at me and I shut my eyes and began to meditate. As soon as I shut my eyes I felt very happy and felt that Bhagavan was very, very near to me and very real and that he was in me. It wasn't like being happy and excited about anything. I don't know what to say, simply very happy and that Bhagavan is so lovely."

And Adam, who was seven, wrote, "When I was sitting in the hall I didn't feel happy so I began to pray and I felt very happy, but not like having a new toy, just loving Bhagavan and everyone."

Not that children sat often or long hours in the hall. When they felt like it they sat; more often they played about.

When Frania, the youngest child, was seven the other two were talking about their friends and she, having no real friends yet but not wanting to be left out, said that Dr. Syed was the best friend she had in the world. Sri Bhagavan was told.

"Ah?" he replied, with perfunctory interest.

And her mother said, 'What about Bhagavan?'

"Ah?" This time he turned his head and showed real interest.

"Frania said, 'Bhagavan is not in the world'."

"Ah!" He sat upright with an expression of delight, placing his forefinger against the side of his nose in a manner he had when showing surprise. He translated the story into Tamil and repeated it delightedly to others who entered the hall.

Later Dr. Syed asked the child where Bhagavan was if not in the world, and she replied, "He is everywhere."

Still he continued in Quranic vein, "How can we say that he is not a man in the world like us when we see him sitting on the couch and eating and drinking and walking about?"

And the child replied, "Let's talk about something else."

And yet any mention of devotees is invidious because there are always others who could be mentioned. For instance, few spoke with Sri Bhagavan more freely than Devaraja Mudaliar or than T.P. Ramachandra Aiyar, whose grandfather had once taken the young Sri Ramana by main force to a ceremonial meal in his house — the only house in which he ever took food after his arrival at Tiruvannamalai. Many beautiful pictures of Sri Bhagavan, showing incredible variety of expression, were taken by Dr. T.N. Krishnaswami, who used to come on occasional visits from Madras. Some of the most vivid and delightful accounts of incidents at the Ashram, breathing the charm of Sri Bhagavan's presence, are contained in letters written in Telugu by a lady devotee, Nagamma, to her brother D.S. Sastry, a bank

manager at Madras. Again, there were devotees who seldom or
never found it necessary to speak to Sri Bhagavan. There were
householders who came whenever occasion permitted from
whatever town or country their destiny had placed them in and
others who paid one short visit and remained thenceforth
disciples of the Master though not in his physical presence. And
some there were who never saw him but received the silent
initiation from a distance.

Sri Bhagavan discouraged anything eccentric in dress or
behaviour and any display of ecstasy. It has already been shown
how he disapproved of the desire for visions and powers and
how he preferred householders to strive in the conditions of
family and professional life. He evoked no spectacular changes
in the devotees, for such changes may be a superstructure without
foundation and collapse later. Indeed, it sometimes happened
that a devotee would grow despondent, seeing no improvement
at all in himself and would complain that he was not progressing.
In such cases Sri Bhagavan might offer consolation or he might
retort, "How do you know there is no progress?" And he would
explain that it is the Guru not the disciple who sees the progress
made; it is for the disciple to carry on perseveringly with his
work even though the structure being raised may be out of sight
of the mind. It may sound a hard path, but the disciples' love
for Bhagavan and the graciousness of his smile gave it beauty.

Any exaggerated course such as *mouna* or silence was also
discouraged. On at least one occasion Sri Bhagavan made this
very clear. Hearing that Major Chadwick intended to go *mouni*
next day, he spoke at length against the practice, pointing out
that speech is a safety valve and that it is better to control it than
to renounce it, and making fun of people who give up speaking
with their tongue and speak with a pencil instead. The real *mouna*

is in the heart and it is possible to remain silent in the midst of speech just as it is to remain solitary in the midst of people.

Sometimes, it is true, there was exaggeration. In accordance with the concealed nature of his *upadesa*, explained in a previous chapter, Sri Bhagavan would seldom explicitly bid or forbid, and yet those who embarked on any exaggerated course must have felt his disapproval, even if they did not admit it to themselves, for they almost invariably began absenting themselves from the hall. I recollect one such case where the mental balance was threatened and Sri Bhagavan said explicitly, "Why does she not come to me?" One has to know how scrupulously he avoided giving explicit instructions or telling anyone to come or go, how skilfully he parried any attempt to manoeuvre him into doing so, how binding and how precious the slightest indication of his will was considered, in order to appreciate the significance of such a saying.

In this case the devotee did not come and shortly afterwards her mind was unhinged. This was not the only instance. Despite the air of normality, the terrific force radiating from Sri Bhagavan was too potent for some who came. It was noticeable that, in any such case, as soon as the mental balance had been destroyed the person would cease to seclude himself and begin coming to the Ashram. It was also noticeable that Sri Bhagavan would sometimes scold such a person like a naughty child who had permitted himself some indulgence that he could and should have resisted. In a fairly high proportion of cases, a fight began to be put up under his influence and the sufferer struggled back to normality.

Although such cases have to be mentioned in order to complete the picture, it should not be imagined, from the space bestowed on them, that they were at all frequent. They always remained rare.

It is hard to postulate anything definite about the methods of Sri Bhagavan because exceptions can often be found. There were cases when his instructions were explicit, especially if one could approach him alone. Anantanarayan Rao, a retired veterinary surgeon who had built a house near the Ashram, had several times been summoned urgently to Madras where his brother-in-law was seriously ill. On one occasion he received a telegram to this effect and, although it was late in the evening, took it straight to Sri Bhagavan. Previously he had never paid much attention, but this time he said, "Yes, yes, you must go." And he began speaking of the unimportance of death. Rao went home and told his wife that this time the disease must be fatal. They reached Madras a couple of days before his brother-in-law passed away.

One heard occasionally of more dynamic instances also, such as a devotee being instructed to use the name 'Ramana' as an invocation, but they were never much spoken about.

Usually a devotee would himself take a decision and then announce it tentatively. The deciding was a part of his *sadhana*. If it was rightly done there would be a smile of approval that made the heart sing, perhaps a brief verbal consent. If the decision was not approved that also would usually be visible. A householder once announced his decision to leave Tiruvannamalai for some other town where he could get a better paid job. Sri Bhagavan laughed, "Everyone is free to make plans." The plan did not come off.

When one of India's political leaders went to Madras to hold meetings an attendant who was an admirer of his asked leave to go there. Sri Bhagavan sat with a face like stone, as though he had not heard. Nevertheless the attendant went. He rushed from meeting to meeting, arriving always too late or failing to obtain admission. And when he got back Sri Bhagavan teased him about it. "So you went to Madras without permission? Did you have a successful trip?" So completely devoid of ego was he that he could talk or joke about his own actions as naturally and impersonally as about those of anyone else.

The influence of Sri Bhagavan was to turn one from the pleasure and pain, the hope and anxiety, that are caused by circumstances to the inner happiness that is one's true nature and, realizing this, there were devotees who never asked for anything, even in mental prayer, but strove instead to overcome the attachment that gives rise to wishes. Even though they had not completely succeeded, it would have seemed a sort of betrayal to go to Sri Bhagavan with a request for outer benefits, for anything but greater love, greater steadfastness, greater understanding. If afflictions came, the method was not to seek to get them removed but to ask, 'to whom is this affliction? Who am I?' and thus draw nearer to conscious identity with That which suffers neither birth nor death nor any affliction. And if any turned to Sri Bhagavan with that intention peace and strength would flow into him.

Human nature being what it is, there were also devotees who did ask Sri Bhagavan for help and protection in the events of life. Taking a different point of view, they looked upon him as their father and mother and turned to him whenever any trouble or danger threatened. Either they would write a letter telling him about it or simply pray to him, wherever they might be. And their prayers were answered. The trouble or danger would be averted or, in cases where that was not possible or beneficial, peace and fortitude would flow into them to endure it. Help came to them spontaneously, with no volitional intervention on the part of Sri Bhagavan. That does not mean that it was due merely to the faith of the devotee; it was due to the Grace that emanated from him in response to the faith of the devotee.

Some devotees were puzzled by this use of power without volition and sometimes even without mental knowledge of the conditions. Devaraja Mudaliar has recorded how he once questioned Sri Bhagavan about it.

"If, in the case of Bhagavan as in that of all *Jnanis*, the mind has been destroyed and he sees no *bheda* (otherness) but only the One Self, how can he deal with each separate disciple or devotee and feel for him or do anything for him?" I asked Bhagavan about this and added: 'It is evident to me and many others with me here that when we intensely feel about any of our troubles and appeal to Bhagavan mentally from wherever we happen to be help comes almost instantaneously. A man comes to Bhagavan, some old devotee of his. He proceeds to relate all sorts of troubles he has had since he last met Bhagavan; Bhagavan listens to his story patiently and sympathetically, occasionally even expressing wonder and interjecting, 'Oh! is that so?' and so on. The story often ends: 'When all else failed I finally appealed to Bhagavan and Bhagavan alone saved me.' Bhagavan listens to all this as though it was news to him and even tells others who come later, 'It seems such and such things have happened to so and so since he was last with us.' We know that Bhagavan never pretends, so he is apparently not aware of all that has happened, at least on one plane, until he is told. At the same time, it is clear to us that the moment we are in anguish and cry for help he hears us and sends help in one way or another, at least by giving fortitude or other facilities for bearing the trouble that has descended on us if for some reason it cannot be averted or modified. When I put all this to Bhagavan he replied, 'Yes, all that happens automatically'."

It was very rarely that Sri Bhagavan deliberately used supernatural powers. Moreover if he did so it was as concealed as his initiation and *upadesa*. In the later years there was one householder among the attendants, a Rajagopala Aiyar. He had a son of about three who had been given the name of Ramana, a pleasant little fellow who used to run and prostrate to Sri Bhagavan daily. One evening, after the devotees had dispersed for the night, the child was bitten by a snake. Rajagopala Aiyar picked him up and ran straight to the hall. Even so the child was already blue and gasping by the time he got there. Sri Bhagavan passed his hands over him and said, "You are all right, Ramana." And he was all right. Rajagopala Aiyar told a few of the devotees but it was not much talked about.

Although they shade into one another, a distinction has to be drawn between asking for boons and relying on Sri Bhagavan for one's protection and welfare. The latter he certainly approved of. If any cast the burden of their welfare on him he accepted it. In *Aksharamanamalai* he wrote, depicting the attitude of the disciple to the Guru: "Didst Thou not call me in? I have come in and my maintenance is now Thy burden." He once, on the request of a devotee, selected forty-two verses from the *Bhagavad Gita* and arranged them in a different sequence to express his teaching, and among them was the verse, "I undertake to protect and secure the welfare of those who, without otherness, meditate on Me and worship Me and ever abide thus attuned." There may be severe trials and periods of faith-testing insecurity, but a devotee who puts his trust in Sri Bhagavan is always looked after.

———————

16

THE WRITTEN WORKS

THE ENTIRE WRITINGS of Sri Bhagavan are very small in bulk, and even of them (then) nearly all were written to meet the specific needs of devotees. Devaraja Mudaliar records in his diary how Sri Bhagavan remarked on this when speaking about a visiting poet.

"All this is only activity of the mind. The more you exercise the mind and the more success you have in composing verses the less peace you have. What use is it to acquire such accomplishments if you don't acquire peace? But if you tell such people this it doesn't appeal to them; they can't keep quiet. They must be composing songs. . . . Somehow, it never occurs to me to write a book or compose poems. All the poems I have made were on the request of someone or other in connection with some particular event. Even *Forty Verses on Reality*, of which so many commentaries and translations now exist, was not planned as a book but consists of verses composed at different times and afterwards arranged as a book by Muruganar and others. The only poems that came to me spontaneously and compelled me, as it were, to write them without anyone urging me to do so are the *Eleven Stanzas to Sri Arunachala* and the *Eight Stanzas to Sri Arunachala*. The opening words of the *Eleven Stanzas* came to me one morning and even though I tried to suppress them, saying 'What have I to do with these words?' they would not be suppressed till I composed a song bringing them in; and all the words flowed easily, without any effort. In the same way the second stanza was made the next day and the succeeding ones the following days, one each day. Only the tenth and eleventh were composed the same day."

He went on to describe in his characteristically vivid way how he composed the *Eight Stanzas*.

"The next day I started out to go round the Hill. Palaniswami was walking behind me and after we had gone some way Aiyasami seems to have called him back and given him a pencil and paper, saying, 'For some days now Swami has been composing poems every day. He may do so today as well, so you had better take this paper and pencil with you.'

"I learnt about this only when I noticed that Palaniswami was not with me for a while but caught me up later. That day, before I got back to Virupaksha, I wrote six of the eight stanzas. Either that evening or the next day Narayana Reddi came. He was at that time living in Vellore as an agent of Singer & Co. and he used to come from time to time. Aiyasami and Palaniswami told him about the poems and he said, 'Give them to me at once and I will go and get them printed.' He had already published some books. When he insisted on taking the poems I told him he could do so and could publish the first eleven as one form of poem and the rest, which were in a different metre, as another. To make up the required quota I at once composed two more stanzas and he took all the nineteen stanzas with him to get them published."

Many poets composed songs to Sri Bhagavan in various languages, outstanding among them being Ganapati Sastri in Sanskrit and Muruganar in Tamil. Although, in the conversation quoted above, Sri Bhagavan deprecated the writing of poetry as a dissipation of energy that could be turned inwards to *sadhana*, he listened graciously and showed interest when poems were sung before him. Prose books and articles about him were also written, and he would often have them read out and translated so that all could understand. One was struck by the extraordinary impersonality of his interest, the childlike innocence of it.

There are two prose books which one might say were written by Sri Bhagavan. During the early years at Virupaksha, when he was still maintaining silence, he wrote out instructions on various occasions for Gambiram Seshayyar, and after Seshayyar's death these were arranged and published as a book under the title *Self-Enquiry*. Similarly, his replies given at the same period to Sivaprakasam Pillai were amplified and arranged in book form as *Who Am I?* The other prose books that the Ashram has published were not written by him but are records of verbal expositions that he gave in answer to questions and are therefore all in the form of dialogue.

His poems fall into two groups: those which express rather the approach through *bhakti*, that is through love and devotion, and those which are more doctrinal. The first group is composed of the *Five Hymns to Sri Arunachala* all written during the Virupaksha period. The element of devotion in them does not imply any abandonment of Advaita but is perfectly fused with Knowledge. They were written from the standpoint of the aspirant or devotee, even though he who wrote them was in fact established in the supreme Knowledge, in the Bliss of Union not the pain of longing; and it is for this reason that they appeal so powerfully to the heart of the devotee.

Mention has already been made of two of them, the *Eight Stanzas* and the *Eleven Stanzas*. In the latter Sri Bhagavan not only wrote as an aspirant but actually used the words, "One who has not attained the Supreme Knowledge." Desiring an explicit confirmation, one of the devotees, A. Bose, asked him why he wrote so, whether it was from the standpoint of the devotees and for their sake, and Sri Bhagavan admitted that it was so.

The last of the *Five Hymns* Sri Bhagavan wrote first in Sanskrit and then translated into Tamil. The story of its writing is astounding. Ganapati Sastri asked him to write a Sanskrit poem, and he replied, laughing, that he did not know the fundamentals of Sanskrit grammar or any Sanskrit metres. Sastri explained a metre to him and implored him to try. The same evening he composed five perfect verses in Sanskrit. They have been rendered into English as follows:

Ocean of nectar, full of Grace, engulfing the universe in Thy Splendour, Oh Arunachala, the Supreme! Be Thou the Sun and open the lotus of my heart in Bliss.

Oh Arunachala! in Thee the picture of the universe is formed, abides and is dissolved. In this enigma rests the miracle of Truth. Thou art the Inner Self Who dancest in the hearts as 'I'. 'Heart' is Thy name, Oh Lord!

He who turns inward with untroubled mind to search where the consciousness of 'I' arises realizes the Self and rests in Thee, Oh Arunachala! as a river when it merges in the Ocean.

Abandoning the outer world, with mind and breath controlled, in order to meditate on Thee within, the Yogi sees Thy Light, Oh Arunachala! and finds his delight in Thee.

He who dedicates his mind to Thee and, seeing Thee, always beholds the universe as Thy form, who at all times glorifies Thee and loves Thee as none other than the Self, he is the Master without peer, being one with Thee, Oh Arunachala! and lost in Thy Bliss.

These stanzas are more doctrinal than the other four hymns, epitomising as they do the three main *margas* or approaches to realization. Speaking about them later, Sri Bhagavan explained: "The third stanza deals with the *Sat* aspect (Being), the fourth with *Chit* (Consciousness) and the fifth with *Ananda* (Bliss). The *Jnani* becomes one with the *Sat* or Reality like a river merging in the ocean; the Yogi sees the light of *Chit*; the *bhakta* or karma yogi is immersed in the flood of *Ananda*."

However, the most moving and beloved of the *Five Hymns* is the *Marital Garland of a Hundred and Eight Verses to Sri Arunachala*, commonly known in English by its refrain, 'Arunachala Siva'. During the early years of Sri Bhagavan's abode at Virupaksha, Palaniswami and others used to go into town to beg food for the small group of devotees, and one day they asked Sri Bhagavan for a devotional song to sing as they went. He replied that there were plenty of sublime songs composed by the Saints, many of them neglected, so there was no need to compose a new one. However, they continued to urge him and some days later he set out on *pradakshina* round the Hill, taking a pencil and paper with him, and, on the way, composed the hundred and eight verses.

Tears of ecstasy streamed down his face as he wrote, sometimes blinding his eyes and choking his voice. The poem became the great devotional inspiration of the devotees. All the pain of longing and all the bliss of fulfilment are mirrored in its glowing symbolism. The perfection of Knowledge is combined with the ecstasy of devotion. And yet this most heartfelt of poems was composed from the standpoint of the devotee, of one who is still seeking. It is also an acrostic, its hundred and eight verses beginning with the successive letters of the Tamil alphabet. Nevertheless, no poem could be more spontaneous. Some devotees asked Sri Bhagavan the interpretation of some of the verses and he replied: "You think it out and I will too. I didn't think while I was composing it; I just wrote as it came."

There is an ancient legend that a party of Rishis or Sages, living with their families in a forest, were practising karmas, that is ritualistic and devotional acts and incantations, by which they had attained supernatural powers and hoped eventually to obtain the supreme Deliverance. In this, however, they were mistaken. In order to convince them of their error, Siva appeared before them as a mendicant, accompanied by Vishnu in the guise of Mohini, a beautiful lady. All the Rishis fell in love with Mohini and their wives with Siva, with the result that their equanimity was disturbed and their powers began to wane. Seeing this, they decided that Siva must be an enemy and conjured up serpents, and a tiger and elephant that they sent against him. Siva, however, merely took the serpents for a garland and, slaying the tiger and elephant, used the skin of the former as a loincloth and of the latter as a shawl. The Rishis thereupon, recognising his greater power, bowed down before him and besought him to give them *upadesa* or guidance. Only then did Siva explain to them their error, teaching that action cannot bring release from action, that karma is the mechanism, not the cause of creation, and that it is necessary to go beyond action to contemplation.

The poet and devotee Muruganar wrote this story in Tamil verse, but when he reached the point where Siva gives instruction to the Rishis he besought Bhagavan, who was Siva Incarnate, to write it. Thereupon Bhagavan composed the *Upadesa Saram* or *Instruction in Thirty Verses* in which, beginning with devout and disinterested activity, he explains that, beneficent as this is, incantations are more effective, silent incantations again more effective than those uttered aloud, and more effective still contemplation. Sri Bhagavan translated the Thirty Verses into Sanskrit and the Sanskrit version is regarded as a scripture in that it was chanted daily before Sri Bhagavan together with the Vedas and is now so chanted before his samadhi shrine of grace.

The doctrine taught by Sri Bhagavan is enunciated the most comprehensively in this poem and in the *Ulladu Narpadu* or *Forty Verses on Reality* together with its *Supplement* of a second forty verses.

Many translations have been made of the *Forty Verses on Reality* and commentaries written on it. It has a universality and a condensed wisdom that demands commentary. And yet, as Sri Bhagavan remarked in the conversation quoted above, it was not written as a continuous poem but the verses were composed from time to time as occasion arose. Some of the supplementary forty were not even composed by Sri Bhagavan himself, but culled from other sources, for when an adequate verse existed elsewhere he saw no need to write a new one. Nevertheless, the whole is the most complete and profound enunciation of his doctrine.

Apart from these two groups there are a few short poems also. Humour is not lacking among them. One contains instructions for *sadhana* under the symbolism of a recipe for making *poppadum*, a favourite South Indian savoury. The mother of Sri Bhagavan was making it one day and asked him to help, and he thereupon spontaneously wrote the symbolical recipe for her.

The poet Avvayar once wrote a complaint against the stomach: "You will not go without food even for one day, nor will you take enough for two days at a time. You have no idea of the trouble I have on your account, Oh wretched stomach! It is impossible to get on with you!"

One day there had been feasting at the Ashram and all were feeling more or less uneasy, and Sri Bhagavan parodied Avvayar's stanza. "You will not give even an hour's rest to me, your stomach. Day after day, every hour, you keep on eating. You have no idea how I suffer, Oh trouble-making ego! It is impossible to get on with you."

It was in 1947 that Sri Bhagavan wrote his last poem. This time it was not in response to any request, and yet it had something of the appearance of a *tour de force*, since he wrote it first in Telugu, but to a Tamil metrical form, and then translated it into Tamil. It was called *Ekatmapanchakam* ('Five verses on the Self').

> Forgetting the Self, mistaking the body for the Self, going through innumerable births and finally finding and being the Self — this is just like waking up from a dream of wandering all over the world.

He who asks 'Who am I?' although existing as the Self, is like a drunken man who asks about his own identity and whereabouts.

When in fact the body is in the Self, to think that the Self is within the insentient body is like thinking that the cinema screen on which a figure is projected is inside the figure.

Has the ornament any existence apart from the gold (of which it is made)? Where is the body apart from the Self? The ignorant mistake the body for the Self, but the *Jnani*, knower of the Self, perceives the Self as the Self.

That one Self, the Reality, alone exists for ever. If even the Primal Guru (Adi Guru, Dakshinamurti) revealed it in silence, who can convey it in speech?

There are also a few translations, mainly from Shankaracharya. A visitor to Virupaksha Cave once left there a copy of Shankaracharya's *Vivekachudamani*. After looking through it, Sri Bhagavan recommended Gambiram Seshayya to read it. He, however, did not know Sanskrit, so he wanted it in Tamil. Palaniswami obtained a loan of a Tamil verse rendering and Seshayya, seeing it, wrote to the publishers for a copy but was told that it was out of print. He therefore asked Sri Bhagavan to make a simple rendering in Tamil prose. Sri Bhagavan began to write one but before he had got far with it Seshayyar received the verse edition he had ordered, so he left the work uncompleted. A few years later, on the earnest request of another devotee, he took up the work again and finished it. Only then did the devotee say that his purpose in pressing for its completion had been to get it published. Hearing this, Sri Bhagavan wrote a preface saying that a free prose version might be of use even though a Tamil verse rendering already existed. The preface itself contains an epitome of the book and a concise exposition of doctrine and the path.

The last thing he ever wrote was a Tamil translation of Shankaracharya's *Atma Bodha*. It had been with him in Virupaksha in the very early days but he had never thought of translating it. In 1949 a Tamil translation, perhaps not a very perfect one, was sent to the Ashram, and shortly afterwards Sri Bhagavan himself felt the urge to make one. For some days he ignored it, but the words of the translation rose up before him, verse by verse, as though already written, so he asked for paper and pencil and wrote them down. So completely effortless was the work that he said, laughing, that he was afraid some other author might come along and claim that the work was really his and had been copied.

Also among the works of Sri Bhagavan is a compilation of forty-two verses from the *Bhagavad Gita* which, on the request of a devotee, he selected and rearranged to express his teaching. This has been translated into English under the name *The Song Celestial*.

17
MAHASAMADHI

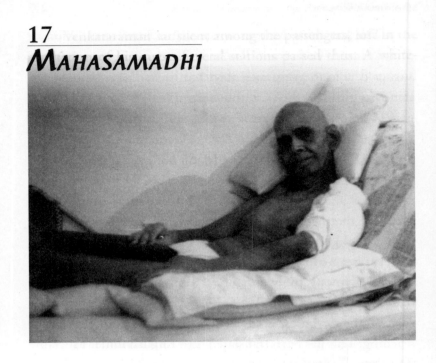

FOR SEVERAL YEARS before the body's end, at least from 1947 onwards, the health of Sri Bhagavan had caused alarm. Rheumatism had not only crippled his legs but attacked his back and shoulders also. Even apart from that, there was an impression of great weakness, although he himself refused to take notice of it. It was felt that he needed a more nutritious diet than the Ashram food, but he would not consent to take anything extra.

He was not yet seventy but looked much more aged. Not careworn, for there was absolutely no sign of care — he had known none. Just aged and very frail. Why was it that one who had been vigorous and robust, who had known little sickness in life and no grief or care, should have aged so much beyond his years? He that taketh upon himself the sins of the world — he who alleviates the karma of the devotees — it was only by himself drinking the poison churned up that Siva could save the world from destruction. Sri Shankara wrote: "Oh Sambhu,[1] Lord of life! Thou bearest also the burden of Thy devotees' temporal life."

There were many signs, always inconspicuous, how, even physically, Sri Bhagavan bore the burden. A devotee, Krishnamurthi by name, has related in a Tamil journal issued by Janaki Ammal, a lady devotee, how he went and sat in the hall one day when he had a severe pain in the index finger. He told no one, but to his surprise, he saw Sri Bhagavan hold and rub the same finger on his own hand, and the pain disappeared. Many others have known similar relief.

For Sri Bhagavan life on earth was no treasure to be economised; it was indifferent to him how long it lasted. There was once a discussion in the hall as to how long he would live. Some quoted the astrologers as saying that he would live to be eighty; others either denied the accuracy of astrology or doubted its applicability to Sri Bhagavan who had no more karma to work out. He listened to the discussion, smiling but taking no part in it.

A newcomer, puzzled by this, asked, "What does Bhagavan think about it?" He did not reply but smiled approvingly when Devaraja Mudaliar replied for him, "Bhagavan does not think about it." The whole last year of his life was an illustration of this. The devotees grieved over the suffering and dreaded the threatened death; he did not.

Early in 1949 a small nodule appeared below the elbow of his left arm. It was not considered serious, but in February the

---

[1] A name for Siva.

Ashram doctor cut it out. Within a month it returned, larger and more painful, and this time it was recognised as a malignant tumour and caused general alarm. Towards the end of March doctors came from Madras and operated. The wound did not heal up properly and the tumour soon began to grow again, larger and higher up.

Henceforth there was an air of tragedy and inevitability about the march of events. The orthodox medical men let it be known that they could not cure the tumour but could only operate and that it might return again, despite radium treatment and, if it did, would eventually prove fatal. Those of other schools believed that they could cure it and that operating would only bring it back in a worse form, as in fact happened, but they were not allowed to try in time.

When the tumour returned after the March operation the doctors suggested amputating the arm, but there is a tradition that the body of a *Jnani* should not be mutilated. Indeed, it should not be pierced with metal and even the operation had been a breach of tradition. Sri Bhagavan had submitted to that but he refused the amputation. "There is no cause for alarm. The body itself is a disease; let it have its natural end. Why mutilate it? Simple dressing of the part is enough."

His saying "there is no cause for alarm" led to the hope that he would recover, despite the words that followed and despite the medical opinion; but for him death was no cause for alarm.

He also gave rise to hope by saying, "Everything will come right in due course." But in fact it was for us to perceive the rightness of what occurred; he never doubted it.

About this time he translated into Tamil verse a stanza from the *Bhagavatam* (*Skanda* XI, ch. 13, *sloka* 36), "Let the body, the result of fructifying karma, remain still or move about, live or die, the Sage who has realized the Self is not aware of it, just as one in a drunken stupor is not aware of his clothing."

Some time later he expounded a verse from the *Yoga Vasishtam*: "The *Jnani* who has found himself as formless pure Awareness is unaffected though the body be cleft with a sword. Sugarcandy does not lose its sweetness though broken or crushed."

Did Sri Bhagavan really suffer? He said to one devotee: "They take this body for Bhagavan and attribute suffering to him. What a pity!" And to one of the attendants he said, "Where is pain if there is no mind?" And yet he showed normal physical reactions and normal sensitivity to heat and cold, and a devotee, S.S. Cohen, records him as having said years earlier, "If the hand of the *Jnani* were cut with a knife there would be pain as with anyone else but because his mind is in bliss he does not feel the pain as acutely as others do." It is not that the body of the *Jnani* does not suffer injury but that he does not identify himself with the body. The doctors and some of the attendants were convinced that there was pain and that, in the later stages, it was excruciating. Indeed, the doctors were amazed at Sri Bhagavan's indifference to pain, at his complete unconcern, even during an operation.

The question of his suffering, like the question of our karma, exists only from the point of view of duality; from his point of view, the point of view of Advaita, neither had any reality. It was with this meaning that he said more than once to devotees, "I am only ill if you think I am; if you think I am well I shall be well." So long as a devotee believed in the reality of his own body and its suffering, so long, for him, the body of the Master was real and suffered also.

For a week or two after the March operation a village herbalist was allowed to try his treatment, but it brought no cure: Sri Bhagavan said to another aspirant who was passed over, "I hope you don't mind when you have taken so much trouble with your medicines." It was never any thought of his own condition, only consideration for those who wished to treat him and loyalty to whatever doctor was in charge. Occasionally he protested at the amount of attention bestowed on his body. Several times when there seemed to be an improvement he declared that he wanted no more treatment.

The tumour, diagnosed now as a sarcoma, sapped his little remaining vitality; and yet even as he weakened his face grew gentler, more gracious, more radiantly beautiful. At times his beauty was almost painful to behold.

The arm was heavy and inflamed and the tumour growing. Occasionally he would admit "there is pain" but he would never say "I have pain." In August a third operation was carried out and the wound treated with radium in the hope of destroying the affected tissues and preventing the return of the tumour. The same afternoon, a few hours after the operation, Sri Bhagavan was so gracious as to sit on the veranda of the dispensary where it had been performed, so that the devotees could file past and have *darshan*. One could see that he was exhausted but there was no sign of suffering in his face. I had come for the day from Madras, and as I stood before him the radiance of his smile was such that even exhaustion ceased to be visible. At noon next day he returned to the hall so as not to inconvenience other patients by occupying the dispensary.

There was also a deeper sense of inevitability, far beyond the medical: that Sri Bhagavan knew what was appropriate and sought to give us strength to endure his body's death. Indeed, this long, painful sickness came to appear as a means of preparing us for the inevitable parting which many had first felt they would not be able to endure. Kitty, who was at a boarding school in the hills, was told about it in a letter and wrote back, "I am so very sorry to hear about it, but Bhagavan knows what is best for us." Her letter was shown to him and his face was radiant with pleasure as he commended her wisdom for saying, "What is best for us", not "What is best for him".

He had immense compassion for those who grieved over the suffering and he sought to appease their grief, not the easy way by removing the suffering and postponing death for a few more years, but the fundamental way by making them realize that the body was not Bhagavan. "They take this body for Bhagavan and attribute suffering to him. What a pity! They are despondent that Bhagavan is going to leave them and go away — where can he go, and how?"

For some weeks after the August operation there seemed to be an improvement, but in November the tumour appeared again, higher up the arm, near the shoulder. In December the fourth and last operation was carried out. The wound from this never healed. The doctors admitted now that they could do no more. The case was hopeless, and if the tumour returned again they could only administer palliatives.

Jayanthi fell on January 5th, 1950. Sorrowful crowds gathered for this his seventieth birthday, which most now felt to be his last. He gave *darshan* and listened to many new songs composed in his praise. Some he read through. The temple elephant from town came and bowed down before him and touched feet with its trunk. A Rani from North India was allowed to take a motion picture of the scene. There was festivity but with an underlying sadness of apprehension.

Many felt already that it was a matter of weeks or days. Now that the case had been pronounced hopeless Sri Bhagavan was asked to say himself what treatment should be tried. He said: "Have I ever asked for any treatment? It is you who want this and that for me, so it is for you to agree about it among yourselves. If I were asked I should always say, as I have said from the beginning, that no treatment is necessary. Let things take their course."

Only after this homeopathy was tried and then ayurveda, but it was too late.

Sri Bhagavan kept to his normal daily routine until it became physically impossible. He took his morning bath an hour before sunrise, sat up to give *darshan* at fixed hours, morning and evening, went through the Ashram correspondence and supervised the printing of Ashram publications, often making suggestions. After January he became too weak to sit in the hall and give *darshan*. A small bathroom with an ante-room had been constructed across the drive just east of the hall and towards the end he remained there. There was a narrow little veranda outside where his couch was put and right up to the end the devotees whom his sickness had drawn in their hundreds to Tiruvannamalai still had *darshan*. He would let nothing interrupt this so long as it was still possible. The devotees would sit morning and afternoon on the hall veranda facing him. Later, when he had grown too weak for that, they would file past the open door of his room, morning and evening. One day his condition caused alarm and the *darshan* was stopped, but as soon as he was able to take notice he expressed displeasure and ordered it to be resumed.

A group of devotees daily chanted prayers and devotional songs for his recovery. He was asked about their efficacy and replied, smiling, "It is certainly desirable to be engaged in good activities; let them continue."

The tumour returned just above the unhealed wound. It was up near the shoulder now and the whole system was poisoned, so that severe anaemia set in. The doctors said the pain must be terrible. He could take scarcely any nourishment. Occasionally he was heard to moan in his sleep but he gave no other sign of pain. From time to time the doctors came from Madras to see him and he was courteous and hospitable as ever. Right up to the end his first question was whether they had received food, whether they were well looked after.

His sense of humour also remained. He would joke about the tumour as though it was something that did not concern him. A woman, in her grief, beat her head against a pillar near the room and he looked surprised and then said, "Oh, I thought she was trying to break a coconut."

Speaking to the attendants and to T.N. Krishnaswami, doctor and devotee, he explained: "The body is like a banana-leaf on which all kinds of delicious food have been served. After we have eaten the food from it do we take the leaf and preserve it? Do we not throw it away now that it has served its purpose?"

On another occasion he said to the attendants: "Who is to carry this load of a body even after it needs assistance in everything? Do you expect me to carry this load that it would take four men to carry?"

And to some of the devotees: "Suppose you go to a firewood depot and buy a bundle of firewood and engage a coolie to carry it to your house. As you walk along with him he will be anxiously looking forward to his destination so that he can throw off his burden and get relief. In the same way the *Jnani* is anxious to throw off his mortal body." And then he corrected the explanation: "This exposition is all right as far as it goes, but strictly speaking even this is not quite accurate.

The *Jnani* is not even anxious to shed his body; he is indifferent alike to the existence or non existence of the body, being almost unaware of it."

Once, unasked, he defined *Moksha* (Liberation) to one of the attendants. "Do you know what *Moksha* is? Getting rid of non-existent misery and attaining the Bliss which is always there, that is *Moksha*."

It was hard to give up hope that even if the doctors failed he might still put aside the sickness by his own power. A devotee begged him to give but a single thought to the desirability of getting well, as this would have been enough, but he replied, almost scornfully, "Who could have such a thought!"

And to others who asked him simply to will his recovery he said, "Who is there to will this?" The 'other', the individual that could oppose the course of destiny, no longer existed in him; it was the 'non-existent misery' that he had got rid of.

Some of the devotees made it a plea for their own welfare. "What is to become of us without Bhagavan? We are too weak to look after ourselves; we depend on his Grace for everything." And he replied, "You attach too much importance to the body," clearly implying that the end of his body would not interrupt the Grace and guidance.

In the same vein he said: "They say that I am dying but I am not going away. Where could I go? I am here."

Mrs. Taleyarkhan, a Parsi devotee, besought him: "Bhagavan! Give this sickness to me instead. Let me bear it!" And he replied, "And who gave it to me?"

Then who gave it to him? Was it not the poison of our karma?

A Swedish sadhu had a dream in which the afflicted arm opened and he saw there the head of a woman with grey hair dishevelled. This was interpreted to mean that it was the karma of his mother that he assumed when he gave her *Moksha*, but others saw the woman to signify all mankind or Maya itself.

On Thursday, April 13th, a doctor brought Sri Bhagavan a palliative to relieve the congestion in the lungs but he refused it. "It is not necessary; everything will come right within two days."

That night he bade his attendants go and sleep or meditate and leave him alone.

On Friday the doctors and attendants knew it was the last day. In the morning he again bade them go and meditate. About noon, when liquid food was brought for him, he asked the time, punctual as ever, but then added, "But henceforth time doesn't matter."

Delicately expressing recognition of their long years of service, he said to the attendants, "The English have a word 'thanks' but we only say *santosham* (I am pleased)."

In the morning the long crowd filed past the open doorway silent with grief and apprehension, and again between four and five in the evening. The disease-racked body they saw there was shrunken, the ribs protruding, the skin blackened, it was a pitiable vestige of pain. And yet at some time during these last few days each devotee received a direct, luminous, penetrating look of recognition which he felt as a parting infusion of Grace.

After *darshan* that evening the devotees did not disperse to their homes. Apprehension held them there. At about sunset Sri Bhagavan told the attendants to sit him up. They knew already that every movement, every touch was painful, but he told them not to worry about that. He sat with one of the attendants supporting his head. A doctor began to give him oxygen but with a wave of his right hand he motioned him away. There were about a dozen persons in the small room, doctors and attendants.

Two of the attendants were fanning him, and the devotees outside gazed spell-bound at the moving fans through the window, a sign that there was still a living body to fan. A reporter of a large American magazine moved about restlessly, uneasy at having been impressed despite himself and determined not to write his story till he got away from Tiruvannamalai to conditions that he considered normal. With him was a French press-photographer.

Unexpectedly, a group of devotees sitting on the veranda outside the hall began singing 'Arunachala-Siva' (*Aksharamanamalai*). On hearing it, Sri Bhagavan's eyes opened and shone. He gave a brief smile of indescribable tenderness. From the outer edges of his eyes tears of bliss rolled down. One more deep breath, and no more. There was no struggle, no spasm, no other sign of death: only that the next breath did not come.

For a few moments people stood bewildered. The singing continued. The French press-photographer came up to me and asked at what precise minute it had happened. Resenting it as journalistic callousness, I replied brusquely that I did not know, and then I suddenly recalled Sri Bhagavan's unfailing courtesy and answered precisely that it was 8.47. He said, and I could hear now that he was excited, that he had been pacing the road outside and at that very moment an enormous star had trailed slowly across the sky. Many had seen it, even as far away as Madras, and felt what it portended. It passed to the north-east towards the peak of Arunachala.

After the first numbness there was a wild burst of grief. The body was carried out on to the veranda in a sitting posture. Men and women crowded up to the veranda railing to see. A woman fainted. Others sobbed aloud.

The body was placed garlanded upon a couch in the hall and the devotees thronged there and sat around it. One had

expected the face to be rocklike in *samadhi*, but found it instead
so marked by pain that it gripped one's heart. Only gradually
during the night did the air of mysterious composure return
to it.

All that night devotees sat in the large hall and townsfolk
passed through in awed silence. Processions streamed from the
town and back singing 'Arunachala-Siva'. Some of the devotees
in the hall sang songs of praise and grief; others sat silent. What
was most noticeable was not the grief but the calm beneath it,
for they were men and women deprived of him whose Grace
had been the very meaning of their life. Already that first night
and much more during the days that followed, it became clear
how vital had been his words: "I am not going away. Where
could I go? I am here." The word 'here' does not imply any
limitation but rather that the Self is, that there is no going, no
changing, for That which is Universal. Nevertheless, as devotees
felt the inner Presence of Bhagavan and as they felt the continued
Divine Presence at Tiruvannamalai, they began to regard it as a
promise full of love and solicitude.

During the night of vigil a decision had to be taken as to the
burial. It had been thought that the body might be interred in
the new hall, but many devotees opposed the idea. They felt that
the hall was, in a sense, an adjunct to the temple and would make
the shrine of Sri Bhagavan seem subordinate to that of the Mother,
reversing the true order of things. Next day, by general agreement,
a pit was dug and the body interred with divine honours in the
space between the old hall and the temple. The crowd, packed
tight, looked on in silent grief. No more the beloved face, no
more the sound of his voice; henceforth the lingam of polished
black stone, the symbol of Siva, over the samadhi was the outer
sign, and inwardly his footprints in the heart.

18
CONTINUED PRESENCE

THE CROWDS DISPERSED and the Ashram seemed an abandoned place, like a grate with the fire gone out. And yet there was not the wild grief and despair that has so often followed the departure of a Spiritual Master from earth. The normality that had been so pronounced still continued. It began to be apparent with what care and compassion Sri Bhagavan had prepared his devotees for this. Nevertheless, during those first days and weeks of bereavement few cared to remain at Tiruvannamalai, and some who would have cared to could not.

Some of those whose devotion sought expression in action formed a committee to manage the Ashram. Niranjanananda Swami consented to work with them, and they, for their part, consented to accept him as the permanent president of the

Committee. Others formed groups or *sabhas* in the various towns they lived in, holding regular meetings.

Unfortunately, it cannot be said that there were none who made trouble or tried to gain prominence for themselves; that always happens when a Spiritual Master leaves the body, but at least there were few such and most of the devotees remained steady.

Many years previously a will had been drawn up stating how the Ashram was to be run when the Master was no longer bodily present. A group of devotees took this to Sri Bhagavan and he read it through very carefully and showed approval, after which they all signed as witnesses. Briefly, it stated that puja (ritualistic worship) should be performed at his samadhi and that of the mother, that the family of Niranjanananda Swami's son should be supported, and that the spiritual centre of Tiruvannamalai should be kept alive. There were attempts later to draw up some different kind of will but Sri Bhagavan would never consider it.

It is the third item that is the great legacy and obligation. The devotees are contributing thereto according to their nature and capacity. Some there are who do no more than sit in silent meditation or who merely come when circumstances permit to receive consolation and pour out the devotion and gratitude of their heart. They are disciples of the Master who said, "Lectures may entertain individuals for hours without improving them; silence, on the other hand, is permanent and benefits the whole of mankind." Even though their meditation falls short of the tremendous spiritual silence of Bhagavan, it not only receives but transmits his Grace and is bound to have effect. And if several worship or meditate together the effect is cumulative.

Others by speech or writing help to set in train an interest which may ripen into a deeper understanding.

Those who are drawn more to outer activity have the burden of organisation upon them, which also is a *sadhana* and acceptable to Sri Bhagavan only when performed as such. They hope eventually to erect a hall of meditation. At present there is a simple stone samadhi surmounted by a lingam and covered over with palm-leaf roofing, between the temple and the old hall.

Everywhere his Presence is felt, and yet there are differences of atmosphere. Morning and evening there is *parayanam* (chanting of the Vedas) before the samadhi, as there used to be before his bodily presence, and at the same hours. As the devotees sit there in meditation it is the same as when they sat before him in the hall, the same power, the same subtlety of guidance. During *parayanam*, puja is performed at the samadhi and the 108 names of Bhagavan are recited. But in the old hall is a softer, mellower atmosphere breathing the intimacy of his long abidance. Some months after the *Mahasamadhi* (leaving the body) this hall was damaged by a fire that broke out, but was fortunately not destroyed.

There is also the little room where the last days and hours were spent. A large portrait which hangs there seems to live and respond to devotion. Here are the various objects that Sri Bhagavan used or touched — his staff and water vessel, a peacock fan, the revolving bookcase, many little objects. And the couch now forever empty. There is something infinitely poignant, inexpressibly gracious about the room.

In the new hall a statue of Sri Bhagavan has been installed. It was one of the terms of the will that a statue should be set up, but no sculptor has yet been found to make one adequate. He would have to feel the mystery of Sri Bhagavan, to be inspired by him, for it is not a question of rendering human features but the divine power and beauty that shone through them.

Not only the Ashram premises are hallowed but all the neighbourhood around. The peace that abides there encompasses and permeates: no passive peace but a vibrant exhilaration. The very air is redolent with his Presence.

True, his Presence is not confined to Tiruvannamalai. It never was. The devotees, wherever they may be, find his Grace and support, his inner Presence, not merely as potent but even more potent now than before. And yet, now as before, the solace of a visit to Tiruvannamalai sinks into the soul and residence there has a beauty hard to describe.

There have been Saints who have promised to return to earth for the renewed guidance of their devotees in life after life, but Sri Bhagavan was the complete *Jnani* in whom there is not even that vestige of an ego that may indicate rebirth, and the devotees understood this. His promise was different. "I am not going away. Where could I go? I am here." Not even "I shall be here" but "I am here", for to the *Jnani* there is no change, no time, no difference of past and future, no going away, only the eternal 'Now' in which the whole of the time is poised, universal, spaceless 'Here'. What he affirmed was his continued, uninterrupted Presence, his continued guidance. Long ago he had told Sivaprakasam Pillai, "He who has won the Grace of the Guru shall undoubtedly be saved and never forsaken," and when devotees spoke during the last sickness as though he was forsaking them and pleaded their weakness and continued need of him he retorted, as already mentioned, "You attach too much importance to the body."

They quickly discovered how true this was. More than ever he has become the Inner Guru. Those who depended on him feel his guidance more actively, more potently now. Their thoughts are riveted on him more constantly. The *vichara*, leading to the Inner Guru, has grown easier and more accessible. Meditation brings a more immediate flow of Grace. The repercussion of actions, good and bad alike, is more swift and strong.

After the first shock of bereavement devotees began to be drawn back to Tiruvannamalai. It is not only the introspective type who feel the continued Presence. One devotee, Dr. T. N. Krishnaswami, believed himself to be bound to Sri Bhagavan only by personal love and devotion and said sorrowfully after the *Mahasamadhi*, "For people like me everything is finished." A few months later, returning from a visit to Tiruvannamalai, he said, "Even in the old days there was never such peace and beauty there as now." And it is not only the introspective type who feel the continued inner guidance; it is an immediate response to devotion.

The devotees were always like a large family, but now a stronger sense of fellowship grew (has grown) up among them. They met in the old hall and discussed the teachings of Sri Bhagavan and exchanged reminiscences, bringing to light their experiences and sayings of Sri Bhagavan which none felt the need to speak about formerly.

The mystery of Arunachala Hill also has become more accessible. There were many formerly who felt nothing of its power, for whom it was just a hill of rock and earth and shrubs like any other. Mrs. Taleyarkhan, a devotee mentioned in the previous chapter, was sitting once on the Hill with a guest of hers, talking about Sri Bhagavan. She said: "Bhagavan is a walking God and all our prayers are answered. That is my experience. Bhagavan says this Hill is God Himself. I cannot understand all that, but Bhagavan says so, so I believe it." Her friend, a Muslim in whom the courtly Persian traditions of culture still lingered, replied, "According to our Persian beliefs I would take it as a sign if it rained." Almost immediately there was a shower and they came down the Hill drenched to tell the story.

But from the time when the Spirit left the body and a bright star trailed towards the Hill devotees have felt more directly that it is holy ground; they have felt in it the mystery of Bhagavan.

Ancient tradition has it that Arunachala Hill is wish-fulfilling and pilgrims have gone to it through the centuries with prayers for boons; but those who feel its peace more deeply do not wish, for the way of Arunachala is the way of Bhagavan that sets one free from wishes, and that is the great fulfilment.

"When I draw near, looking upon Thee as having form, Thou standest as a Hill on earth. He who seeks Thy form as formless is like one travelling over the earth in search of formless space. To dwell without thought upon Thy nature is to lose one's identity like a sugar doll immersed in the ocean. When I come to realize who I am, what else (but Thee) is this identity of mine. Oh Thou who standest as the towering Aruna Hill?" (from the *Eight Stanzas on Sri Arunachala*).

It is not only those who have been before and have seen the beauty of Sri Bhagavan in his bodily form who feel the attraction. Theirs is an inestimable fortune but others also are drawn to him, to Arunachala. It will be enough to mention two such. Miss Howes had been waiting fourteen years for a possibility of going, after reading Paul Brunton's *A Search in Secret India*. Circumstances made it possible only after the *Mahasamadhi*. She gave up her job and sold her effects to raise the necessary funds. She was able to stay only a few weeks; however, feeling the Grace of his Presence, she said: "I thought

I should be disappointed when I knew he was dead, but I wasn't. It was worth it, every moment of it. Now I can only look forward to the day when I shall come back again."

Coming back is in the hands of Bhagavan. Now, as before, he draws to himself and to Tiruvannamalai whom he will. Miss Howes was confident from past experience that she would have no difficulty in finding a new job when she got back, but this time it did not happen so. Week followed week with nothing suitable turning up. Then she heard of a good vacancy, was interviewed and told that she could have the job if she wanted but that it was in India. So her return was made easy.

Dr. D.D. Acharya retired after a long and successful practice in Central India and decided to dedicate the evening of his life to spiritual quest. He travelled over India, visiting one temple or ashram after another, without finding the peace he sought, until he came to Tiruvannamalai. Immediately he felt, 'this is home', and he settled down there as the Ashram doctor.

After some time he fell into despondency, as others have done before, at seeing no improvement in himself and wept before the samadhi, "Why did you bring me here, Bhagavan, if you are not going to give me the peace I seek?"

That same night he saw in a dream Bhagavan seated on his couch and, approaching, knelt before him. Sri Bhagavan took the bent head in his hands and asked what he was grieving about. Then, in answer to the complaint, he replied, almost as he had to other devotees during his lifetime, "It is not true that you are making no progress; it is I who know that, not you."

Dr. Acharya pleaded eagerly: "But I must attain realization now, in this life! Why should I wait? Why should it go so slowly?"

And Sri Bhagavan laughed. "That is your destiny (*prarabdhakarma*)."

In this dream by one who had never seen Sri Bhagavan in his lifetime, the replies were such as he would then have made. Just as formerly, it was less the words spoken that were reassuring than the indescribable charm of his solicitude.

Others also will come. Ananda Mayi Ma, a well-known woman Saint of North India, came to the samadhi and, refusing a seat of honour prepared for her, said: "Why all this fuss? I have come to pay homage to my Father and can sit on the ground with the others." A South Indian woman Saint was asked by Mrs. Taleyarkhan about herself and others still living in the body and replied, "He was the Sun and we are its rays." The story is no more ended than the story of Christ was ended upon the cross. It is, indeed, not a new religion that Sri Bhagavan brought upon earth, but a new hope, a new path, for those who understand and aspire from every land and religion in this age of spiritual darkness. It was not for his body's lifetime only. To those who feared that the guidance might end with death he replied curtly, "You attach too much importance to the body." Now, as then, he guides whoever approaches him and whoever submits to him he supports. To all who seek he is here.

———————

GLOSSARY

Abheda	:	No-otherness (see *bheda*).
Adi-Guru	:	The ancient or primordial or original Guru. The Divine Source from which the power of initiation and guidance descends to a line of Gurus. An epithet of Sri Shankaracharya and sometimes also of Dakshinamurti.
Adina-Guru	:	The founder of a line of Gurus. Except in the case of the founder of a new path, initiation (like ordination) is valid only when given by one who is duly authorised and whose authorisation goes back in an unbroken chain to the founder of his line.
Advaita	:	Non-duality, the doctrine that nothing exists apart from the Spirit, but everything is a form assumed by the Spirit (see the third paragraph of Chapter IX).

The principal doctrinal division among the Hindus is between the schools of Advaita and Dvaita. The Dvaitists or Dualists worship a Personal God separate from the worshipper. The Advaitists, while recognising the truth of this conception on its own plane, go beyond it to the conception of the Absolute in which a man is absorbed back into That which is his Source and real Self, surviving in the pure Bliss and boundless Consciousness of Being.

Ajnana	:	Ignorance. The prefix 'a' (as in *abheda*) is a negative, so the word literally means 'lack of knowledge'.
Ananda	:	Bliss, beatitude.
Anugraham	:	Grace.
Ardra Darshan	:	*Ardra* (*Arudra*) literally means 'wet'. Siva's birth star is *Ardra* signifying the Lord's overflowing compassion for his devotees. Siva granted *darshan* to Patanjali, Vyaghrapada and others on this day. Hence its importance. Sri Bhagavan was born on the night of this day at 1 a.m. under the star *Punarvasu* — that is, the star next to *Ardra*, which was the presiding star during the day. Both the stars are under the constellation of *Mithuna* (Gemini).
Arunachaleswar	:	God in the form of Arunachala, a contraction of Arunachala-Iswara.
Ashram	:	The establishment or colony that grows up around a Sage or Guru; sometimes mistranslated as 'monastery'.
Ashtavadhana	:	The ability to attend to eight different matters simultaneously.
Asramam	:	The Tamil form of 'ashram'.
Asuric	:	Diabolical, evil.
Atma or *Atman*	:	The Spirit or Self.
Atmaswarupa	:	Literally the 'form of the Spirit'; a term used for the universe to indicate that the universe has no intrinsic reality but exists only as a manifestation of the Spirit.

Avatar	:	An incarnation or manifestation or Vishnu, that is of God as the Preserver and Sustainer of the universe. Within the manvantara or cycle stretching (according to Christian symbolism) from the Earthly Paradise (the state of Adam before the fall) to the Heavenly Jerusalem (the consummation after the second coming of Christ) there are ten Avatars. The seventh is Rama, commemorated in the *Ramayana*, a Sanskrit epic; the eighth is Krishna, commemorated in the *Bhagavad Gita*; the ninth is described as the non-Hindu Avatar and is identified as Buddha or Christ or both, the tenth is Kalki, the destroyer of sin with whose coming the *Kali Yuga* or dark age is to be ended. He is still to come and is equivalent to the second coming of Christ awaited by the Christians and Muslims and the Maitreya Buddha of the Buddhists.

Sometimes the term Avatar is used more loosely to indicate a divine manifestation. |
Ayurveda	:	The traditional Hindu system of medicine.
Bhagavad Gita	:	Literally the 'Divine Song' or, more correctly, 'God-Song', since 'Bhagavad' is a noun used adjectivally. The scripture of Sri Krishna, the eighth Avatar, probably the most widely studied and followed Hindu scripture. It occurs as an episode in the Sanskrit epic, the *Mahabharata*.
Bhagavan	:	The same word as 'Bhagavad' with a different case-ending; the commonly used word for

'God'. Terms such as Iswara, Brahma, Vishnu, Siva and names for the various aspects of God are more technical or philosophical. In ordinary conversation a man says either 'Bhagavan' (God) or 'Swami' (the Lord).

The term 'Bhagavan' is used by general consent for those few supreme Sages who are recognised as being completely One with God.

Bhakta	:	Devotee. Also one who approaches God through love and devotion.
Bhakti-marga	:	The approach to God through love and devotion.
Bhakti	:	Love or devotion.
Bheda	:	Otherness. The difference between *bheda* and *abheda* is substantially the same as that between *dvaita* and *advaita*. The exponent of *bheda* regards himself as 'other than God', whereas the exponent of *abheda* regards God as the Absolute or Infinite apart from which there can be no other.
Bhiksha	:	An offering of food to the Guru or to a sanyasin. In the case of Bhagavan this came to mean providing an ashram meal, since he would accept nothing that was not shared by all.
Brahma	:	Iswara, Personal God, is conceived of under the threefold aspects of Brahma, the Creator, Vishnu, the Preserver, and Siva, the Destroyer. There are temples to Vishnu and Siva but not to Brahma, as man is concerned with God as

Preserver or God as Destroyer of forms in the Bliss of Union rather than with God as Creator.

Brahman : The highest and ultimate conception, the Absolute, about which nothing can be postulated, since any assertion would be a limitation. The first stage in the manifestation of Brahman is Iswara, the Personal God.

Brahmin : The Hindus were divided traditionally into four castes, of whom the Brahmins were the highest, being devoted to a life of spirituality and study. Next came the Kshatriyas, who were the rulers, warriors and administrators. The Vaishyas were the middle classes and the Shudras the labourers. The castes were not at first exclusively hereditary, but since each caste married within itself, even the law of heredity made them so practically. In course of time they became strictly so and also subdivided into hereditary sub-castes, largely on a professional basis, like mediaeval guilds in Europe. Also they tended to abandon their caste functions and engage in those of other castes. Today caste has little functional meaning. The Indian government is trying to destroy it.

Chakra : The yogic and tantric paths (see *marga*) unfurl the spirit-force in man (kundalini) from its latency at the base of the spine and cause it to ascend through a series of spiritual centres in the body. Each of these is called a disc or *chakra*. Each represents a different stage of development which is franchised as the kundalini attains it.

Chela   :   Disciple.

Chit   :   Consciousness. (see *Satchitananda*)

Daivic   :   God-like or Divine. An English adjectival form from *deva*, meaning angel or holy spirit.

Dakshinamurti : Siva manifested in ancient times as a youth who taught in silence, initiating and guiding his disciples by direct transmission of the Spirit. He is particularly associated with Arunachala, the centre of silent and purely spiritual initiation and guidance, and therefore also with Sri Bhagavan, who was Siva teaching in silence.

Darshan   :   Literally 'sight'. Since one speaks of a holy man giving darshan, it could best be translated as 'silent audience'. To have darshan of a Sage could be translated as to enjoy the grace of his presence.

Dharma   :   Harmony, harmonious life or action. Also a man's role in life, since what is harmonious conduct for one (say, a soldier) may not be so for another (say, a priest).

Dhoti   :   A white cotton cloth that Hindu men in South India wear. It is wound round the waist and hangs down like a skirt from waist to ankles.

Diksha   :   Initiation.

Giripradakshina: *Pradakshina* is the circuit that is made of any holy place, walking round with one's right side inward, that is from south to west. *Giri* is a hill; so *giripradakshina* is used for circuit of Arunachala.

Guru	:	Spiritual guide or Master. For the various grades of meaning see page 165.
Jnana	:	Knowledge, Divine Wisdom or Understanding. Spiritual Enlightenment.
Jnana-marga	:	The Path of Knowledge. This does not mean a path requiring great theoretical elaboration but one based on intuitive knowledge or spiritual understanding (see *Marga*).
Jnani	:	A Man of Knowledge. It may be used to mean one who follows the *Jnana-marga*, but in its correct meaning it is one who has attained complete Enlightenment and is established in the Absolute Knowledge which is liberation from all illusion of duality. It thus means the same as *Mukta*, the liberated or perfectly realized man.
Iswara	:	The Personal God. (see under Brahma)
Japa	:	Invocation or incantation.
Jayanthi	:	Birthday.
Kali Yuga	:	The Dark Age, equivalent to the Iron Age of Graeco-Roman traditions, said to have begun in 3101 B.C. with the Battle of Kurukshetra, that is with the teaching of Sri Krishna recorded in the *Bhagavad Gita* and to be now approaching its end (see *Yuga*).
Karma	:	The destiny that a man makes for himself by the law of cause and effect. There are three kinds of karma: *prarabdha*, or that which is to be worked out in this life,

sanchitha, or that which existed at the beginning of this life but is held over, and *agamya* or the new karma which is accumulated in this life and added to the *sanchitha*. (See the first paragraph of Chapter X.) The law of karma combines the two theories of predestination and cause and effect, since a man's present actions cause or predestine his future state.

Karma also means action. It is sometimes used to mean ritualistic actions performed as a *marga* or path to salvation.

Just as karma is accumulated by a man's actions and desires, so it can be destroyed by divine love and knowledge and by renunciation of desires. Therefore it is said that karma is like a mountain of gunpowder that can be burnt up by a single spark of *Jnana* (Divine Knowledge).

Karma-marga : The approach to God through harmonious and disinterested actions, that is, as is said in the *Bhagavad Gita*, by acting without being attached to the fruits of one's actions, doing one's duty simply because it is one's duty, not for profit or ambition, and not being deflected from it by fear or favour. This is normally accompanied by ritualistic acts.

Kavyakanta : One whose speech is like poetry. A brilliant improvisor of poetry.

Krishna	:	The eighth Avatar. The Divine Teacher whose doctrine is contained in the *Bhagavad Gita*.
Kumbhabhishekam:		Consecration.
Lingam	:	An upright pillar of stone often used to represent Siva or the Absolute on the grounds that any image or idol is limiting and therefore misleading. The word comes from *linga*, to get absorbed, and the root meaning is 'that in which all beings are absorbed'.
Maharshi	:	Maha Rishi, the Great Rishi or Sage. The name is used for one who opens a new path to Realization. It is also a name of Vishnu as the fountain-head of initiation and paths to Realization.
Mahasamadhi	:	The great or final or complete *samadhi* or absorption in the Self or Spirit. The term is sometimes used for the physical death of a great Saint, but for the Maharshi even this is inappropriate since he was already in *Mahasamadhi* while wearing a body, and the body's death made no difference to him.
Mantapam	:	A shrine or bare stone hall, with or without the image of a God inside.
Mantra	:	A sacred formula used as an incantation.
Mantradhyana	:	Meditation or spiritual awareness induced or supported by the use of incantations.
Marga	:	Mode of approach in the spiritual quest. Basically, there are three *margas*: the *Jnana-marga*, *bhakti-marga* and *karma-marga*.

Jnana-marga is the approach through Knowledge or understanding, by which is meant not mental but spiritual knowledge. Physical knowledge is direct, as when you burn your finger and know pain; mental knowledge is indirect, as when you know that fire burns; spiritual knowledge is again direct, though quite different.

Bhakti-marga is the approach through love and devotion to God.

Karma-marga is the approach through harmonious and disinterested activity.

The three *margas* are not mutually exclusive. There can be no spiritual knowledge without love. Also, love and devotion to God leads to understanding and to Union, which is Knowledge. For activity to be perfectly harmonious and disinterested it must be inspired by love and understanding. *Jnana-marga* leads to disinterested activity free from the thought: 'I am the doer of this and should have the praise or reward for it.'

Bhakti-marga leads to dedicated activity, seeing God manifested in all his creatures and serving him by serving them.

Nevertheless, although the *margas* merge and all lead to the same goal, they start from different points and their methods are different in practice.

Apart from the three basic *margas*, there are two less direct and more elaborate developments of *Bhakti-marga*, that is the yogic and tantric paths. They are very far from the teaching of Bhagavan and need not be described here.

Math   : A private temple or shrine, something like the chantries of Mediaeval England.

Matrubhuteswara: God (*Iswara*) in the form of the Mother.

Maulvi (Arabic): A Muslim learned in Islamic doctrine and law. The Islamic equivalent of a pandit.

Moksha   : Liberation or Deliverance. Salvation is generally used in a dualistic sense to mean the salvation of a purified soul in the presence of God; *Moksha* is used in the complete and ultimate sense of liberation from all ignorance and duality through realization of identity with the Self.

Mouna   : Silence.

Mouna diksha : Initiation through silence (see pp. 171-2).

Mouni   : One who has taken a vow of silence.

Mount Meru   : The mountain which, in Hindu mythology, is the Spiritual Centre of the universe. Bhagavan affirmed that Arunachala is Mount Meru.

Mukta   : One who has attained *Moksha* or Deliverance. One who attains *Moksha* during the life on earth is sometimes called *Jivanmukta*, that is '*Mukta* while living'.

Mukti   : Deliverance; the same as *Moksha*.

Muni   : Sage.

Nataraja   :   A name for Siva. Siva in the cosmic dance of creation and destruction of the universe.

Nirvikalpa samadhi: Samadhi in a state of trance, with suspension of the human faculties (see page 45).

Nishkamyakarma: Action without attachment to the outcome, that is without egoism. Action which does not create new karma.

OM   :   The supreme mantra, representing the substratum of creative sound which sustains the universe. It is written with the three letters AUM but pronounced OM.

Pandit   :   One learned in the Hindu scriptures, doctrines and law. Sometimes transliterated 'pundit'.

Paramatman   :   The Supreme Atma or Spirit. Actually, the word Atma itself is often used in this sense and was so used by Bhagavan.

Parayanam   :   Singing or chanting.

Pial   :   A raised platform or stone or concrete couch often built outside a Hindu house or in the porch of it.

Pradakshina   :   See *Giripradakshina*.

Prana   :   Breath or vital force.

Pranayama   :   Breath-control, either regulating or suspending breathing.

Prarabdha   :   See karma.

Prarabdhakarma: See karma.

Prasadam   :   Some object given by the Guru as a vehicle of his Grace. When food is offered to the

		Guru it is usual for him to return a part of it as *prasadam*.
Puja	:	Ritualistic worship.
Pujari	:	One who performs puja.
Purana	:	Mythological scriptural story carrying a symbolical meaning.
Purusha	:	The Spirit. Atma is used in the pure sense of Spirit, whereas *Purusha* is used more in the masculine sense where Spirit is contrasted or coupled with Substance (*Prakriti*). In common speech it can be used for 'man' or 'husband'.
Rishi	:	Sage, literally Seer.
Rudra	:	A name for Siva as He who proclaims himself aloud.
Rupa	:	Form.
Sadhaka	:	Spiritual aspirant or seeker.
Sadhana	:	Spiritual quest or path. The technique of spiritual effort.
Sadhu	:	This word should correctly mean one who has attained the goal of *sadhana* but is in fact used for one who has renounced home and property in the quest, whether there is attainment or not.
Sahaja Samadhi	:	Continuous *samadhi* not requiring trance or ecstasy but compatible with full use of the human faculties. The state of the *Jnani* (this term is not used traditionally but used only by Sri Bhagavan).

Saivite   :   From the point of view of Siva. A devotee of Siva. The main division in Hinduism is between Saivism and Vaishnavism, the standpoints represented by Siva and Vishnu respectively. This corresponds to the difference between *Advaita* and *Dvaita*, since the devotees of Vishnu stop short at duality, while Saivism is the doctrine of non-duality. It also corresponds to the difference between *Jnana-marga* and *Bhakti-marga*, since the Advaitist proceeds by spiritual understanding and the Dvaitist by love and devotion to God.

These differences are not similar to those between Christian sects, since both paths are recognised as legitimate and a man follows whichever suits his temperament.

Sakti   :   The Force, Energy or Activity of a Divine Aspect or Principal. In Hindu mythology a Divine Aspect or Principle is represented as a God and its Energy or Activity as the Consort of Siva.

Samadhi   :   (1) Absorption in the Spirit or Self, with or without trance and suspension of the human faculties.

(2) The tomb of a Saint. Sometimes any tomb is so described.

(3) A euphemism for death. Instead of saying that someone died it is customary to say that he attained samadhi.

Samatva	:	The practice of treating all equally, with like consideration, seeing all alike as manifestations of the Spirit.
Sambhu	:	A name of Siva, Siva as the Bounteous.
Samsara	:	The endless chain of births and deaths to be broken only by Self-realization. Human life. The cares and burdens of life. *Samsaram* — commonly used in Tamil to mean 'wife'.
Sankalpas	:	Inherent tendencies, desires and ambitions.
Sanyasin	:	One who has renounced home, property, caste and all human attachments in the spiritual quest. The renunciation is permanent and definitive, whereas a sadhu is free to return to family life. A sanyasin wears the ochre robe as a badge of renunciation, whereas a sadhu wears a white dhoti.
Sari	:	The normal attire of women in most parts of India. The lower half is wound round the body like a skirt and the upper half taken up and draped over the left shoulder.
Sarvardhikari	:	Master or ruler.
Sastraic	:	Based on or in accordance with the Sastras. The Sastras are scriptural rules governing conduct, art, science, government, etc.
Sat	:	Pure Being. (See *Satchitananda*).
Satchitananda	:	Literally Being-Consciousness-Bliss. A term for the Divine State, since spiritually to know is to be, and to know or be the Self is pure Bliss.

Sadguru   : The Guru of Divine power as distinguished from guru in a more limited sense (see page 165).

Sattvic   : The universe is brought into being and maintained in equilibrium by the combined action of the three *gunas* (stresses, tensions or tendencies), *sattva*, *rajas* and *tamas*. *Tamas* is the movement downwards from Spirit to matter, from Unity to multiplicity; *rajas* is the expansion outwards into activity and multiplicity; *sattva* is the ascent to the Spirit.

Cosmically, the *gunas* are neither good nor evil but simply the mechanism of manifestation; however, in a human being *tamas* is the tendency to evil, malice and ignorance; *rajas* is the tendency to outer activity; *sattva* is the tendency to spirituality, involving freedom from worldly passions and attachments. 'Sattvic' and 'unsattvic' are English adjectival forms used respectively of anything that aids or impedes spiritual effort.

Sattya-Yuga   : The golden age (see *Yuga*).

Shahada (Arabic): The Islamic creed: La ilaha ill' Allah, "There is no god but God".

Siddha   : This may mean one who has attained Self-realization but is commonly used to mean one who has supernatural powers whether or not he has spiritual attainment.

Siddha Purusha: A Sage (embodied or disembodied) possessing supernatural powers.

Siddhi   : Supernatural powers.

Siva : In the simple theoretical sense Siva may be regarded (see under Brahma) as an aspect of Iswara (the Personal God). However, to his devotees Siva is the Destroyer of the prison walls in which the Spirit of man is held, the Destroyer of the ego, of the duality of man and Iswara, of all limitations, leaving only Absolute Being, which is perfect Knowledge and pure Bliss. Therefore Siva is the Absolute personified, containing Iswara and all the gods and worlds as a dream within himself.

Sivaswarupa : The form of Siva; a name sometimes given to the universe to indicate that it has no intrinsic reality but exists only as a form assumed by Siva.

Sri : Blessed or beatific. In modern times it is often used as a form of address, almost equivalent to 'Mr.'; however, it is still applied in its true sense to a Saint.

Sruti : Scriptural text.

Suddha Manas : Purified, sattvic mind.

Swami : Lord. It is used to mean 'the Lord' in speaking of God; also for a spiritual master or teacher whether or not he has attained any higher state; sometimes also as a mere sign of respect.

Swarupa : One's true form.

Taluq (Urdu) : A local governmental district.

Tao : In Chinese teaching 'Tao' is used both for the path (*sadhana*) and the Goal, that is the Self or Absolute (Atma).

Tapas : Penance or austerity. For a fuller explanation see page 44.

Tirtha : Sacred tank.

Upadesa : The instruction or guidance given to a disciple by his Guru.

Vairagya : Dispassion, detachment.

Vasanas : Latencies or tendencies inherent in a man, resulting from his actions in a previous life and governing those in this life unless overcome by tapas or by the Grace of his Guru.

Vedas : The earliest Hindu scriptures, revealed to the ancient Rishis.

Vichara : Discrimination. The path of Self-enquiry taught by Sri Bhagavan, since this path implies discrimination between the Real and the unreal, the Self and the ego.

Vijnana : Specialised knowledge. Knowledge of the Self and also of the outer world.

Vishnu : God in His Aspect of Preserver and Sustainer of the universe.

Yoga : Literally 'Union'. An indirect approach (see *Marga*) which starts from the standpoint of duality and seeks to develop a man's latent powers by very technical means, with the final object of attaining Divine Union.

Yogi : One who follows or has mastered the path of yoga.

Yuga : Age. According to Hindu, as to Graeco-Roman and Mediaeval, teaching there are four ages in the *manvantara* or cycle from the 'Earthly Paradise' of Adam before the fall to the 'Heavenly Jerusalem' or consummation after the tenth Avatar (see Avatar). They are called the Satya Yuga (Age of Truth or Purity), Dwapara Yuga (Second Age), Treta Yuga (Third Age) and Kali Yuga (Dark Age). Their duration is said to be in the proportion of 4: 3: 2: 1, so that the Kali Yuga is one-tenth of the entire *manvantara*.